Other Books by Stuart Wilde

Miracles
The Force

AFFIRMATIONS

BY STUART WILDE

WHITE DOVE INTERNATIONAL, INC.
P.O. BOX 1000, TAOS NM 87571
USA (505)758-0500
ISBN - 0-930603-02-8

© Copyright 1987 by Stuart Wilde
Printed in the USA by Bookcrafters

First printing July 1987
Second printing September 1987

"Life was never meant to be a struggle; just a gentle progression from one point to another, much like walking through a valley on a sunny day."

Stuart Wilde

Firstly, I dedicate this work to ol' B-D, without whose valuable assistance I could have finished this book six months ago.

Secondly, I dedicate this book to my good mate, Glynn Braddy, who got me on the path, and who has supported me through thick and thin, these last twelve years.

Thanks, chaps!

CONTENTS

Cover art by Charles Collins, Taos, New Mexico USA
Cover design by Melody, Webb Design, Taos, New Mexico USA
Calligraphy by Joan Machinchick, Lake Clare Design Studio, Annapolis, Maryland USA
Published by White Dove International, Inc., Taos, New Mexico USA

the author

1
SIMPLE BEGINNINGS

I was born when I was very young, in Farnham, England. Conditions at birth were very crowded. My twin sister appeared in the physical plane about twenty minutes ahead of me. I like to think that I allowed her the pole position, being the proper little gent that I was, but if truth be known I was asleep in the wings and missed the curtain call.

My father was an officer in the British Navy. At the time of my birth in 1946, he was seconded to the Foreign Office and served as a diplomat. My mother was Sicilian. They met during the Allied invasion of Sicily and were married in three weeks. She was very bright, a professor of languages and the only person that I have ever known who could speak Latin fluently.

Like many Sicilians she had come to the earth plane to experience "food and emotion." Being crafty, as many Sicilians are, she saved time by combining her evolutionary goals into one event, punching us out emotionally at supper most nights.

But in spite of her imbalances, her capacity to love was endless and so I got off to a good start. During my first decade on earth my parents dragged me around the more obscure parts of the British Empire, while my father administered the Queen's Pleasure, which for the most part seemed to entail requiring the Foreign Office types to spend endless hours standing around ill-lit colonial clubs, drinking gin. As a small boy, I can't say that I really understood how that helped the Queen, but the conversation of the men was so far beyond my comprehension and sounded so important, I presumed that some very secret official business was being done. Anyway, my experiences in those colonial clubs were invaluable for I quickly learnt the ways of the world. The lesson of being exposed to many different cultures helped me develop an open view of the world and its people.

At age ten, disaster struck. I was shipped from a carefree existence on the beaches of Africa to a British boarding school, a mausoleum of a place that was founded in the year dot. Its philosophies were archaic and bizzare to say the least. Much of it could be traced back to some obscure little man who sat on a sand dune in pre-history, developing ways to manipulate and harass people.

I remember clearly my father standing on the tarmac of Accra airport prior to my departure for England, and ceremoniously presenting me with a five pound note ($7.50 at today's exchange rate.) At the tender age of ten that seemed to me an untold fortune. However, once at school I discovered the school sweet shop and through that, along with the ravages of inflation, I experienced my first cash flow crunch about a week-and-a-half into my scholastic career.

Penniless, and six thousand miles from rescue, I affirmed that I would resolve my dilemma. Meanwhile, the professors at school were teaching me all sort of things that they said I would find handy later in life, like "where the Limpopo flows." Somehow, I intuited that the whereabouts of the Limpopo was not going to solve my dilemma and so I set about researching the prime emotional needs of my fellow boarders.

Cigarettes, it seemed, were a prized form of contraband. As ten year old boys we were not allowed out of the grounds, so shortages existed. Demand having been established, I now set about the problem of supply. One morning the gods smiled upon me and I met an older student whose function it was to go to the village on his bike each day to collect the master's newspapers. I pinned him to the wall and in my best Sicilian accent asked him if he would like to go into business. He said, "No." Whereupon I punched him in the nose and we became lifelong friends and partners.

Our import/export business flourished and round about the age of thirteen I had my first taste of my current career as a publisher. Well, not quite. Let me explain. With four hundred boys all reaching puberty at the same time, Thursday afternoon at two fifteen to be precise, girly magazines became all the rage. Luckily enough our capitalization was up to the task and we never looked back. Money flowed from sales and rentals and soon we expanded into the insurance business. For pennies a week a student could insure against getting a beating. Though we could not stop the headmaster from whacking a boy for some transgression of the college rules, the pound note we paid out if he got whacked went a long way to alleviate the pain.

I remember the tennis coach coming up to me on the last day at that school and asking me why I looked so miserable. From within my tears I mumbled, " the business, the business." Graduating from school was my first taste of unemployment.

I mooched around for a few years and wound up as a stage-hand with the prestigious English Stage Company at Sloan Square in London. I had the idea of going into theatre management. My twin sister was by now forging ahead with a showbiz career and was appearing weekly on British TV. However, once I found out that the stage manager earned just forty pounds for a seventy hour work week, the roar of the grease paint and the smell of the crowd lost its allure.

By lying about my age, I got a job as a long distance truck driver and spent a happy year discovering the more forgettable parts of the British Isles, like Barnsley and Accrington. The hours were long but the pay was fair and for the first time in almost ten years I was affirming a personal sense of freedom.

The swinging sixties were hotting up and British rock bands were all the rage. On one of my travels I discovered a textile mill in Lancashire that made a kind of tee shirt vest that miners wore. I bought a few of these and dyed them various colors in my bath. To my amazement the first boutique I offered them to snapped them up. The problem I had was one of logistics. I could dye hundreds of tee shirts each day but drying them was a problem. Luckily, they were greatly in demand and in my customers' search for sartorial splendor, they failed to notice that the tee shirt hung limply off the hangers, still slightly wet.

Automation set in. I took on a partner whose main qualification was that he could borrow his father's car. We hired a launderette and ran twenty-six washing machines at once. We were dying thousands of tee shirts per day and scampering to the pub at night to count our winnings. This venture developed into a fully fledged clothing business producing tee shirts, jeans, loon pants and all sorts of wild and wonderful things that no self-respecting hippy could be without.

By the age of twenty, I was earning a little over the sterling equivalent of $20,000 per week. Still no one had asked me where the Limpopo flowed and by now it did not matter if the stupid river had evaporated! I then signed up for a seven year course at the University of Burn-out, cruising London with a group of exotic characters whose names seemed culled from the cockney hall of fame. My chauffeurs were called Billy the Kid and Slick Vic, and I employed a fellow to get me home safely at night called Richard the Minder. In addition there was a character on the payroll whose sole function it was to keep our "perfumed circus" stoned out of its brains. He was called, appropriately, Hill the Pill.

At the ripe old age of twenty-eight I was exhausted. There were hardly any human experiences left to me. Literally, I had been there, done that, and gotten the tee shirt.

One morning, nursing a terrible hangover, I decided to discover the meaning of life. I signed up to train as a spirit medium at the College of Psychic Studies. I seemed to have a fair talent for it and not long after I was regularly contacting the spirits of the departed in hopes that they might answer my questions as to life's wondrous mysteries.

We would sit in a circle in the dark, and through meditation and introspection we would open up our third-eye. Sure enough symbols or people would appear in the mind. Usually someone's dead Aunt Maude or Uncle Fred would show up for the benefit of one of the sitters. The trick was to give whatever information you saw accurately, not judging it or qualifying it in any way. As I did not have any prior knowledge of the details of the departed spirit's life on earth, it proved to me that I was communicating with the dead. This was more often than not confirmed by someone in the circle who would recognize the details that the spirit energy had given. It was customary at the end of a session to ask the departed spirit if they had any words of encouragement to offer their relatives still in the living. Usually, the dead spirit would say something like, "I know you have had a hard time, duckie, but it will all be alright in three months, and don't forget, God loves ya."

Then sure enough someone's dead Uncle Fred would pitch up, and at the end of that session I would ask for a message and the spirit would say something like, "I know life is hard, mate, but it will all be OK in a couple of months or so, and don't forget, God loves ya." Having delivered a constant stream of relatively inane messages over a period of six months or so, I came to the conclusion that if you are thick as two planks when you are alive, you are thick as two planks when you are dead.

The idea that death grants "all knowing" seems to me a load of baloney, for I have talked to hundreds of dead spirits who would have difficulty directing you to the bus stop! I gave up spirit mediumship and decided to head out into the world in search of someone who knew the answers. On my quest I travelled the equivalent of seventy times round the world, researching every known phenomenon possible. I spent a week in the King's Chamber of the Great Pyramid in Egypt doing EEG experiments on brain wave responses. I investigated hauntings and worked on several spirit possession cases. I looked into ESP, alchemy, tarot, altered states of consciousness, prophesy, levitation, psycho-kinesis, magic, the Kabala and every shade of wild and wonderful thing I could find. I trained for three years with a teacher of eastern mysticism who taught me of the Tao and the necessity of personal discipline, and I fell in with a group of positive European occultists who gave me a knowledge of the esoteric aspects of their ancient tradition.

During those years of searching, I struggled both spiritually and in the worldly sense. If I had only known then what I know now, I could have saved myself much pain and anguish. It was as if my *inner self* were in a life and death battle with my ego or personality. The more I tried to win a higher ground, the more my ego rebelled, flatly refusing to relinquish its dominant position. By setting upon a quest I had pulled away from all the things with which I felt comfortable. In doing so, I began to lose contact with my friends and connections and I went through long periods of intense loneliness and fear. Further, having lost my ability to generate income from my usual sources, I often found myself in periods of acute difficulty. But during those years of turmoil and frustration I constantly held to the dream of reaching a higher perception and I knew that sooner or later I would achieve a break through.

I continued to travel and study endlessly. Many of the sources of knowledge I investigated turned out to be dead-ends, in which I found that the experts really did not know whether they were Arthur or Martha when it came to true knowledge.

Bit by bit I was able to sift the chaff from the wheat and as I worked on myself, my own perceptions began to open up. I developed the ability to enter into deep states of mind and not fall asleep. After five years of training I found that I could hold concentration at the theta brain level (which is 4-6 cycles of brain rhythm per second) almost indefinitely. Eventually I trained myself to hold a theta rhythm and keep my eyes open. This took two more years to perfect.

That was a turning point in my quest, for once I could do that I could see the electro-magnetic force field that surrounds humans. It is not normally visible to the naked eye, but is made up of their feelings about themselves. It is not the aura that psychics or Theosophists talk about, it is more a thumbprint of what the person feels. I would sit in airports for endless hours watching the most intimate details of passers-by. Airports are especially suited for this kind of theta experiment for in airports people are in a heightened state of feeling. The fear of flying and the pressure of travelling cause people to have expanded or exaggerated feelings that allow you to read them more clearly.

This new-found ability caused a tremendous sense of pathos within me for the conditions under which people live. Within their feelings are all their struggles and restrictions along with the limitations they carry with them. You can see quite clearly that most people are living like automatons, "tick-tocking" through life to someone else's tune, in various states of unholy terror or insecurity. This affected me deeply. Ten minutes in any airport and you realize that most people have no clue as to how life works or how they create their destiny or fate.

In my heart I wanted to do something to help, and yet at the same time I was not strong enough myself to be effective and did not really have the courage of my own convictions. Then one day an event occurred that changed my life.

For a year previous to the event, I had been surrounded by many strange phenomena. I had spontaneous clairvoyance; things moved around my house mysteriously; I felt the presence of other worlds. On the day in question, I was walking down the Kings Road Chelsea when a mysterious voice appeared over my left ear and suggested I make a turn down a side street. I obeyed and found myself in front of a library. The voice suggested I walk in. Once inside I paused and was directed to a particular set of shelves. All the books on the shelves were stacked vertically except one which lay horizontally. I felt compelled to select that book.

In it was a post card of Old China, which seemed significant to me as I had been involved in the philosophy of China for a number of years. The book turned out to be the prophesies of Nostradamus and on the page indicated by the card I read, in French, the quatrain numbered 1-76. Loosely translated it says, "There will be a man with a *wild* name, whose function it will be to talk to the world about its fate, and he will do well."

I stood there in the library stunned. I do not think for a moment that Nostradamus knew of my life or that he was writing about me but what shocked me so was the synchronicity of my being in the right place at the right time to receive a message

7

about my life in such a dramatic way. From that day forth I resolved to learn as much as I could about the nature of consciousness and the electro-magnetic field that surrounds us humans, which is so intimately connected with the way our fate unfolds.

A few months after the incident I emigrated to the United States. England had been suffering a gradual economic decline since the time of Harold Wilson, who gave us the philosophy that currently dominates British politics—"equal poverty for all." I had lost interest in money-making and I felt that the relative freedom of the USA would be a welcome change from the restriction I experienced in England.

I ducked into America as a "dry-back," entering as a tourist at Chicago's O'Hare Airport. For a couple of years I lay low, avoiding the immigration people. But my love of the country and the American people was such that I created an affirmation within me that I would survive and eventually I got my immigration paperwork in order.

Meanwhile, I found myself in California. It seemed, in the late Seventies, that there were only two games in town—either you became a guru, or you sold real estate. I opted for real estate as I knew nothing about guruing. I formed a company in Newport Beach with a really neat lawyer called Savage. We titled the enterprise, Savage, Wilde and Company, and somehow the name stuck in people's minds. We made money almost immediately, in spite of the fact that neither Savage nor I had the vaguest clue about real estate. Anyway, we learned as we went along and I sold my shares in the company to Mr. Savage nine months later.

With the nestegg I received I linked up with a metaphysical publishing venture in England and brought it to the USA. Things were hard at first and for a while the venture nearly folded, but gradually the business expanded and after three years it turned a profit. Today it is one of the most wide-spread metaphysical catalog, promotion, and publishing companies in the world, with offices in six countries and a world-wide audience of around ten million.

While the businesses were being developed, I continued my discipline of doing a theta meditation each day. I would wake at four in the morning and would entrance myself for about an hour. For the first three years I watched symbols being released from my inner psyche. Then I entered a period of darkness. I used this time to develop my abilities to concentrate even further, and then one day I had a spontaneous vision of the eternal light.

The beauty of that light is so exquisite that it leaves one short of words with which to describe it. In it is all the compassion you could ever imagine and more, and it has absolutely no judgement or criticism. It comes to us from an infinite perception of time and space and it holds no aspiration or desire for us other than that we learn to love ourselves and that we come to the realization that we, too, are the light and that we, too, have the ability to express the same infinite view.

Shortly after my first view of the light, I discovered in my trance meditations an energy which I eventually came to call the "doorkeeper." The doorkeeper showed me a vision of a place in the United States that he said had a magical power which had existed since before the time of Christ. I had a vague idea what the place felt like but I did not know where it was. The doorkeeper told me I would recognize the location when I found it, because of an energy he called the "Quickening." The whole idea drove me utterly mad! I set about visiting hundreds of locations in the United States in search of the spot.

The doorkeeper said that the power of the Quickening would only be available for a few years and he gave me a symbol with which to recognize it. When I found it, I was to tell no one — not even those close to me — until a certain world event had taken place.

I did not understand what the Quickening was but I felt sure I would know when I found it. One day, visiting friends in Northern New Mexico, I rounded a corner and in front of me was a snow-capped mountain. There was something magical about that place but at first I did not realize that my search had ended. I drove lazily along a high plateau, to my left the sun was setting over a deep gorge. I decided to stop my car and get out to watch the close of another day. As the sun sank slowly behind a group of mountains to the West, I uttered a short Taoist prayer giving thanks for the beauty in all things. The twilight of dusk lay dramatically reflected in the clouds which were surreal streaks of burnt sienna embracing the distant mountains in an infinite kindness. I marvelled at the drama of their shapes and as I looked across the high mesa I noticed that several clouds were forming themselves into an unusual geometric pattern. Minutes later, poised between two peaks was the symbol I had been promised. There, at last, was the Quickening.

A few weeks later, I moved my whole operation to Taos, New Mexico, bought a house and settled down while the doorkeeper gradually explained over a period of two years what the energy of the Quickening really meant.

As an individual turns inward and begins to transform his life from the mundane to the celestial, he soon reaches a plateau of comfortableness in which he uses his new found power to materialize all the things he needs. For him to climb from that plateau is extremely difficult, it is comfortable for him to stay there. The Quickening is an energy that allows him to make that final ascent. It is an inner energy that grants man the courage to strive for the quintessence of his evolution.

Nightly, I experimented in the inner worlds, pulling to me teachers who understood the nature of consciousness and the destiny of man and, moreover, who had the symbology to explain things to me in terms I would understand. Meanwhile, I continued to zig-zag back and forth across the physical plane, gaining a solid experience of it.

Not long after reaching Taos, I discovered in my meditations a tunnel or tube. The tunnel, I believe, links the physical plane with other inner dimensions of consciousness. It took me many months to figure a way up the tube, but eventually I adjusted and found that I could enter other worlds almost at will. I believe that this tunnel is the same as that described by people who have near-death experiences, and of my adventures up the tunnel you will read more in a later part of this book.

Years before, in my esoteric studies, I had come across the works of the great Swedish mystic Emanuel Swedenborg. Over a period of seventeen years he had developed the ability to penetrate the electro-magnetic fence that binds human existence and to perceive other worlds. He described the angelic dimensions, along with heaven and hell, in flowery terms, but within the complexity of the way he used language I realized that here was one man who actually knew the secrets of life. I re-read his works and attempted in my nightly experiments to track along the path that he had covered.

Sometimes I was successful, sometimes not, but on the whole I found it relatively simple, and on occasions I discovered areas he had never talked about. As I developed my ability I had spontaneous visions of the "light" and this always inspired me. Eventually, I broke through the barrier so completely that I could see the light almost at will. Swedenborg's work was invaluable to me. What I like about him is that he was a very practical man. He was the minister for mines in his country and wrote hundreds of scholarly texts on geology and mining. He was not given over to wild flights of fancy. I, too, feel that if a philosophy is to work successfully you have to be able to haul it down to the bank on Friday and deposit it.

Over the years I have developed an alternative philosophy which I call *SWAP* (Stuart Wilde's Alternative Philosophy). It is based on my experiences in the light and is under-pinned by my knowledge of the world we live in.

Basically, life was never meant to be a struggle. Yet everything is designed to control us and to limit us. The light (which is truth) is not visible to us, so we make up rules and regulations, partly in an effort to process fear and partly in the hope that we will somehow charm the light into our life. In doing so we restrict ourselves terribly for the light does not come out of do's and don't's—its currency is absolute forgiveness, unbounded compassion, endless patience and love. It expresses this love for us by honoring us in leaving us alone, to be as silly as we want for as long as we want.

Life inside the Circle of life is one of restriction and manipulation and it is through these lessons that we learn to go beyond struggle. Once we discover the power of the light, and providing we do not wrap it in endless mumbo-jumbo, we create for ourselves an alternative evolution, one that takes emotion out of the physical plane to a point where we can control our own destiny.

By using that power, we are able to pull energy from the Universal Mind, which, in turn, gives us a transcendent view that we can use for any endeavor we choose. I believe that, from time to time, men and women like Thomas Jefferson, Einstein, Francis Bacon and Ayn Rand (the author of *Atlas Shrugged*) have understood the simplicity of this power and have used it to exhibit genius.

The metaphysics of this power and these inner worlds is the last known boundary for mankind. Once a person discovers the true nature of realtiy he or she can rightly affirm, "My expectations are truly limitless."

The function of this book *Affirmations* is not to give you nice words to say to yourself; rather, it is to give you a fast track beyond struggle, through understanding the wider meaning of consciousness and reality, thus bringing you into the light.

I am eternal, immortal, universal, and infinite. My expectations are truly limitless.

2
THE ANCIENT WISDOMS

Most of the organizations and structures in the world around you are designed to take away your individual power. This book serves as a magnificent and devastating battle plan, whereby you will learn to expand your personal power and win back absolute control of your life.

The political, social, and financial structures that are imposed upon us today were designed hundreds, if not thousands of years ago. The function of these structures is to influence and control the people, so that they can be manipulated into supporting the system. You have now reached a point in your life where you have enough courage, inner power, and charisma to push against that manipulation and to win back control.

Divesting yourself of the encumbrance of the beliefs of others, you become free. You have to stand alone. That is the only true spiritual path for you. Everything else is just a way station, while you gather enough confidence to step out on your own. You need to get your power back, and fast. To do so you will have to become like a "gorilla on the path" that is going to walk up to the system and lovingly demand its bone back!

But your "power-surge" cannot be achieved through confrontation. Nothing ever comes from blowing up the Town Hall. The sage's way is to discipline himself and to take back his or her power, then wait while the system exhausts itself—which it will. The power brokers of the world have created a system that is careening out of control. In an attempt to enslave the world in debt, they have printed so much phony paper money that the system is on the verge of falling apart. Once that happens, things will change for the better: the individual will have his day, and the intuitive, loving and caring people will inherit the earth.

All you have to do is wait and work on yourself in the mean time. This book outlines your battle plan through heightened perception, discipline, courage and determination. Through it you will create that commanding, transcendent being that calls to you so longingly from within yourself.

Let us start.

There are four main types of affirmations: affirmations of word, affirmations of thought, affirmations of feeling, and affirmations of action.

An affirmation is, in effect, a statement either of word, thought, feeling, or action which underlines or confirms a belief pattern that you hold. There are negative affirmations and positive affirmations.

This book is for those who want to develop and learn how to use affirmations to mold reality to suit their positive ends.

Before discussing in detail what affirmations are and their use, we must look briefly at the ancient wisdoms and at how the Universal Law manifests itself. Those of you who have read *Miracles* and *The Force*, bear with me for a moment as the basic principles are always worth retelling.

Your reality, the situations around you, and the events of your life are created by the energy of your *inner being*. That *inner being* is built of various factors, including every thought, feeling, and action you have ever been a part of. Your *inner being* is strong or weak depending on how you feel about yourself and on how you understand the nature of energy and metaphysical reality.

Every thought or feeling you have about your life, no matter how slight, goes to create the events that are coming towards you. Note that I say "towards you." In the physical plane we accept the illusion that we move towards events. We speak in terms of what will happen next week, or we think about a gift that will arrive in a few days, and in so doing we create a feeling that the future is ahead of us and that we are moving towards it. In fact, the future, metaphysically, is all around us and "events move towards us." Through the laws of attraction you draw situations that exactly reflect your *inner being*.

Whatever you think and feel about your life today is the scaffolding that builds the events you will experience next week or next month. When the time comes, you will fill in the minor details but the main features of the events already will have been created.

This is my day. I control each and every thing that comes to me. I accept complete responsibility for my life. I am power. So be it.

Your thoughts and feelings mingle with the Universal Law and the Law reflects back to you an exact replica of the spiritual you. If you want to know how you are doing, ask yourself this question: "Do I have beauty and abundance around me at all times?" If the answer is yes, your *inner being* is beautiful and its magnificence can be well used.

If, on the other hand, you are surrounded by lack, or if there is negativity in your life, your *inner being* is deprived, and embodies a certain amount of negativity. It is then time for you to "roll up your sleeves," and begin to work on the quality of your life. Affirmation is one of the tools you will use.

There is no situation you cannot change. There is nothing that is beyond your capacity. But first you have to accept total responsibility for your life. Every event, good or bad, is a part of who you are. The event is created solely by you, and there is no other, be it God or some outside force, creating it for you. You and only you are in charge.

Once you accept this unequivocably, you reach a metaphysical maturity that allows you to gain complete control of your life. You learn that there are no accidents, quirks of fate, misfortunes. There is only energy: high energy and not-so-high energy. If a bus turns the corner and runs over your foot, this event comes to you through your lack of balance. It is a lesson from the Universal Law.

By the same token, if a total stranger comes up to you and offers you $10,000, again, it is as a result of the metaphysical energy that you are. Now, you may say, "Such a thing is so unlikely, why would I even bother to think about it?" But the very fact that you are *thinking* about it, allows it to happen. Three years ago, I was thinking that very thought. I had been invited to dinner at the home of a person I had never met. As we waited for the food to be served I talked a little about my life and some of the projects I was working on. Later that evening my host pulled me to one side and offered me $10,000. I accepted.

You could start with the following affirmation: "I am ready, I believe in what I am and I believe in my individuality. Universal Law, give me the wherewithall." Anything you can imagine, anything that you truly can accept as part of your life, exists as a reality in the inner worlds. It may take awhile for the reality you choose to manifest, but if you imagine it—if in your mind you can truly touch, taste, feel and accept it as granted—it becomes part of your life.

The Universal Law is impartial. It will give you anything you believe. It will throw you garbage or roses depending on the energy you put in. You are the one in charge, and you must accept that and stand alone. If you think God is coming down to fix things for you, forget it. God is out playing golf.

Now, if that concept is unacceptable, throw out this book and double your insurance policies. For, in fact, what you are saying or affirming in doing so is, "My life is a game of chance, anything can happen. If I make it through this day it is due to sheer luck." It may sound funny, but people really live like that. They lurch from one crisis to the other and when they get into trouble they pray. More often than not, praying gets them nowhere, but sometimes things change for the better and when they do they say, "God loves me, God saved me."

If you pray to get out of trouble, you draw energy from the emotional feeling or desire to transcend your difficulty. You know what you want, you probably have some ideas about how to solve your problems, and you think and visualize yourself free. And so the Universal Law delivers, providing you believe.

But prayer is not the most effective way of directing energy to your ends. When you pray to an outside force, you express energy away from your self. By doing so you affirm that you are not in control, that something beyond you will fix your problems. It is more effective to turn your energy inward, saying, "I am the power. I pull from within me the energy I need to go beyond my challenges."

You see, God has always been an energy, not a person. At the beginning of the current cataclysmic period, approximately seven thousand years ago, there walked on earth a group of initiates or sages. These individuals had great power. They understood the nature of metaphysical reality, and they taught it to their tribes and followers. However, it is hard for the un-initiated to grasp the true reality of the inner worlds. While the sages lived this did not matter. People experienced the energy through the masters and they had a glimpse of these other worlds, even though their energy was not advanced enough for them to perceive for themselves.

As generations came and went, the initiates died out; the tribes grew and multiplied and some members of the tribes began to move away. In so doing they lost or diluted the spiritual heritage taught by the initiate sages who had led the tribes at the beginning. Unable to perceive the energy themselves, the tribes created gods, and went further to create symbols and statues. Priesthoods grew up so that worship and ritual would be carried out in the correct manner, as dictated by the tribal customs. The priests purported to know the will of God so were able to lead the tribes spiritually and to keep things under control. Since the tribal people believed that an outside force controlled their destiny, they carefully observed the rites, ceremonies and rituals, lest the gods be angered. It was their way of processing fear. Once ritual was established, the notion of sin came into being: if you challenged the will of the priests, or if you failed to support the tribal customs, it followed that you must be acting contrary to the will of God.

Once sin was established in the psyche of the people, the notion of guilt developed. Guilt makes you feel worthless by negating your love of self. The people felt they had less and less power to control their lives. They became weak. And as the people became metaphysically weaker, it followed that the priests and hierarchies assumed more and more power. Theirs was not a real power, but power of the ego, fueled by their pride in being the only ones in the tribe who could communicate with the gods. Eventually, the leaders of the tribes and the common people drifted so far apart metaphysically that the priests and controlling families became identified with the Gods. So the concept of the divine man or solar king developed, a human being so endowed with godliness that he *was* God or at least the prophet of God. This happened not because the leaders were so strong or metaphysically sophisticated, but because the others had fallen into abject weakness.

This weakness pervades our society today. Ritual, sin, fear and guilt are still used to influence the people. This control is thinly disguised but it is there, not only in some of the major religions, but also in the various cults and splinter groups that flourish today. Generally, each group has a king or a leader. He is endowed by his people with divine or semi-divine qualities. In these groups there are laws, patterns, and rituals that have to be followed. Some cults and religions have their own special sayings or language. Each is designed to collect and indoctrinate members in the tribal ways and then use guilt, fear, and obligation, to keep them involved.

At school, I learned Latin and studied the history of the Italians since the time of Christ. After seven years I was theoretically molded in the tribal ways. I could quote the tribal rituals in various languages. I knew the correct vestments to wear on the tribal holy days. I knew exactly what the will of God was and I knew what it was he wanted of me. Of course I knew.

The High Priest had called me to his inner chamber and told me exactly what God wanted of me. I took it all very seriously, for I believed it was real.

It seems that God wanted me to go out into the world and find others who would come and join the tribe and be part of the ritual. God wanted a good percentage growth of new members per annum and he was not going to rest until each and every person in the world had joined the tribe, whether they wanted to or not!

Well, diligent as I was and young, I set out on the task the High Priest had given me. I figured that London would be a good place to start. Eight million people would be a lot of tribal members. The first few people I spoke to there used words I was not too familiar with but from the tone of their voices I understood they were not very interested in joining my mission.

Undaunted, I pressed on. One day at noon a thirst came over me, so I entered a pub. I knew this pub was a den of iniquity, but somehow I felt that contact with the people was important. I had to find out what motivated the populace so that I could win them over to the High Priest's calling.

In the bar I met a young woman from Ireland. She was fresh and unspoiled and she spoke with a lilt in her voice which carried me back to a time when my mother sang to me as a child. I explained my mission to the girl and asked if she would like to join the tribe and take up the tribal ways. I talked to her about my seven years in the institution with the priests and I impressed her with my knowledge of the history of the Italians.

She had come to London from Cork two years before in order to find work and get away from her family. It seems that her father was an ogre. He drank, and she, the youngest of seven children, took the brunt of his ire.

As we sat there enjoying a beer together, she listened diligently to my story, smiling and encouraging me. From time to time she took my hand. Once I caught her looking at me with one of those looks that up to then I had only read about in books. At two in the afternoon the bar closed, and we left together.

We drove to the countryside in an old battered van and climbed a hill that had been sacred to the Druids.

Sitting on the grass overlooking a checkered pattern of English fields, I began to wonder if she would ever consent to join my tribe, for she spoke of everything *but*. And yet I was captivated by her charm and somehow the instructions of the High Priest seemed a long way off.

The girl began to sing a song in her native tongue. It was touchingly beautiful and when she had finished I asked her what it meant. She said it was a song sung by a bird in a cage. The bird was comfortable and loved by its master but the bird was unhappy, for it had all the material things it needed, but it was not free. It longed for the uncertainty of the wild.

We sat in silence for a moment and then the girl asked me a question that changed my life. She asked me if I was truly free. "Of course," I replied defensively, "I am the master of my life." But deep within I knew that I was not free, for rather than enjoying the spontaneity of the moment, the beauty of the girl, the mystery of the Druids' hill, I was troubled, for I was not following the instructions of the High Priest. I feared that the openness and warmth of the girl's gentle ways would surely tempt me down a path as wicked as anything that the tribe might imagine.

Just before sunset, it began to rain. Being somewhat far from the van, we took shelter in a thicket of trees. We walked for a while and came to a bridge that led to a courtyard of an old ruined castle. Little remained of the original structure except a small gatehouse once used by the inhabitants to haul the drawbridge up and down. We entered through an old door, climbed a stone staircase and found ourselves in a small room above what must have been the original drawbridge.

The place overwhelmed me. I could almost hear the courtiers and ladies talking and laughing as they walked about the castle. Time stood still. I felt nervous and self-conscious, and yet all was not lost. The girl took me by the hand and kissed me, and bit by bit, as fast as my courage would allow, she led me down the path all lovers tread: past inhibition, beyond uncertainty, to the door of my lady's chamber.

I never heard from the High Priest, and I am sure that I was ostracized by the tribe. But I had learned freedom. It had only taken me a few days. For some it can take a lifetime.

I wanted to share this story with you, for we all suffer from the control that others place upon us. The things you believe in are the baggage you carry with you in your life. The true sage believes in nothing, other than the sacredness of all things. He lives in the spontaneity of energy. He defends nothing nor judges anything. His world is eternal and infinite, he sees beauty in all things and he accepts the ways of man, including restriction and strife. He knows that without constraints there would be no challenges.

If you are not careful, beliefs can stifle you. Let me elaborate. The people of the world live inside a fence or Circle. That Circle is an electro-magnetic force field created by the oscillations of the neurons in the brain. The force field dominates and alters each man's perception of life and of his physical circumstances. That field of energy cuts man off from perceiving the God Force in all things. He sees only physical reality and he believes that to be real. Moreover, he sees himself separate from that God Force and this robs him of his power.

Because the people in the Circle have no real clue as to the truth behind reality, they have, over the centuries, made up childlike interpretations to explain things to themselves. Many of the world's religions were formulated at a time when people were thick as two bricks! Think of it in terms of one of those religious fanatics who is part of the Middle East today — the cheery kind who blows up people in airports. Now, from whatever that fanatic is today, subtract knowledge, electricity, reading and writing. Then take away from him the benefit of modern communications, travel and medicine and he would be even more slow-witted. Then if you could drag him back two thousand years, denying him the progress the world has achieved in that time, you would have on your hands a total moron in today's terms. That is the intellectual and spiritual level of the people who developed many of the old philosophies. Their perceptions,

I am truly a part of all things. The God Force flows through me. I feel secure.

even within the Circle, were highly restricted, and their perception of reality beyond the Circle was fanatical, tribal and limited by a lack of insight.

Some of those desert philosophies dominate today. They create a further prison that man lives in, by establishing a status quo morality that binds him into a system of bizarre beliefs which he mistakenly feels are real. The power needed to penetrate the Circle and to escape the prison created by those beliefs is so great, that few ever attempt it, and even fewer succeed. Individuals may move from the center of the Circle, which is highly restrictive, to a position nearer the outer edge, which liberates them somewhat. Usually, however, they fall back on the same old habits, replacing one debilitating philosophy for another, or they have no philosophy at all.

That is why I say with certainty that beliefs stifle people, for little of what they believe represents true spiritual reality — it is just simplified representation of that reality. Very few of the beliefs the Circle People hold are original to them. Usually people are imprisoned within a compilation of various bits and pieces of the Circle "mind set" which they accumulate over the years. Then, in believing what they do over a long period of time, the mind set ossifies and hardens around them, and they begin to hold to it as if their life depended on it. In doing so, they are locked in forever.

I believe that the restriction of the Circle is forseen by the *inner you* or Higher Self and that you accepted it lovingly, as you did all the general circumstances of your early life. I believe the Higher Self to be so powerful it has the ability to choose what type of life it wants to experience in the physical. Life on earth is so heroic, and it is such an important evolutionary step, that you did not come here by chance. The ancient idea that God somehow dumped us off and said, "Harass 'em," seems childlike.

When two humans come together in a sexual relationship, they give off an energy that is read by the Higher Self. It chooses the genetic pattern of the babe that it is to be born into and it accepts whatever strengths and weaknesses are to be found within that small body. And so if you were born with one leg shorter than the other, your Higher Self saw that and said, "Fine, I'll take it. Even if I have to experience walking in semi-circles for the rest of my life, I don't care. Get me down there, I need it."

The Higher Self also has the ability to choose the sex and usually selects whichever gender will give it the greatest evolution through the earth plane. So if you are a woman, you are so because you could do "male" standing on your head. You chose womanhood because it does not necessarily come naturally to you. If you are a male you have chosen the awkward task of trying to express strength without infringing on others, and within that strength you have to develop the subtle spirituality of softness.

Before the Higher Self incarnates on earth it can see the future parents as well as the mind set that they adhere to. It scans over to the father, sees that he is a complete Bozo, and says, "Perfect, if I get an image of masculinity from that twit, it will take twenty years to go past that." Then it looks at the mother. There she is with her loving heart, but the Higher Self can see that she is a complete space-cadet. "She's hardly nailed down," says the Higher Self, "Wonderful, it will take me a further twenty years to go past her."

Then the Higher Self looks at what these good people believe. At first it cringes, for it can see that what they believe is completely "wacko," then gradually a smile comes over the Higher Self as it realizes it will take at least another twenty years to transcend that lot. "Perfect," it says, "Twenty years to go past him, twenty to go past her, twenty to overcome what these twits believe, that makes sixty years. Then I'll have ten to myself at the back end. Include me in."

So, you came. You knew it would be the greatest period in the history of man and you could see that, for a while any way, you would be controlled and dominated by others. You could see the restriction of the Circle and you knew that restriction would help you. For from restriction comes eventual freedom. Let us look at the nature of the Circle and see what fun you signed up for.

The Circle is dominated and controlled by approximately two thousand families world-wide. The families are as much a part of the Circle as are the rest of the people. More so, in fact, for the families have a vested interest in the control of mankind and that traps them in the Circle emotionally. In a sub-structure below these powerful families are about twenty-thousand other families and loose knit associations that act as supporters for, or representatives of, the leaders. Two thousand families came to power centuries ago, through force, and they maintain that power today. Do not get me wrong—these families and the associations they formed are not part of the "illuminati," nor are they necessarily evil, they are tight-knit social groups whose sole function is to maintain control. In the societies of Western Europe and North America, the domination they exert on the people is a form of sophisticated manipulation in which they control every aspect of a man's life.

They print the paper money and dictate how much of it a man can have. They set prices and control hourly labor rates, which they pitch at a ceiling that is just above what I call the "revolution level," below which people would take to the street and destroy the very structure the families hope to sustain. It matters not whether you are a manual worker or an executive in a large corporation, the money you are allowed to keep for your efforts only just gets you through. This is because the system is not designed to allow you abundance. When did you last have a couple of hundred thousand lying around unused?

The families control the world banking system and they use the governments which are basically financed and sponsored by them to pass laws regulating every aspect of the financial markets to their favor. The constitution of the United States basically forbids the formation of a central bank. Obviously, the founding fathers in their great wisdom, did not want anyone manipulating the situation. So the families got round that by forming the Federal Reserve System which, of course, is a central bank in everything but name. It prints and controls the flow of money, and sets the price an American pays to borrow that money. In doing so it regulates every aspect of his life. The Federal Reserve System is set up in such a way that it does not answer to the government nor to the people, and so it enjoys a monopoly over the affairs of the most powerful economic trading nation in the world. And because of the immense power of the United States, it imposes its influence on financial markets world-wide. Wouldn't it be nice if you had a part of that? But you do not and, unfortunately, you never will.

The families and their surrogates hold a monopoly on world trade and shipping, and they meticulously control the flow of raw materials basic to human life. In owning most of the world's mining, they have in the past deliberately created shortages of vital goods to sustain inflated markets.

In education their domination is the same. Centuries ago, in Europe, the Christian Church had a monopoly on information and education which they maintained with a vice-like grip through various organizations like the Jesuits. Only the priests, clergy and upper class were permitted education. The common people were deliberately held in ignorance, so that they would not be able to take control. Today, education is still controlled either by the religions or by the status quo and laws are passed to force you to educate your children in the system. That is why the idea of "education of children at home" has received such a battering in recent years. The powers that be do not want you to take your children from their influence.

In addition, the media is used to bombard the people with the "national mind set," molding their attitudes on everything from war, sex and marriage to taxes, as well as on their individual relationship to God and country. Because the journalists and editors pass through the same education system, collecting the same beliefs, they are not much into change. So, we have to be patient. Things will change but it will take time. The result is that the ordinary man or woman is brain-washed into believing that, as an individual, he or she has to support the status quo, and pay for the privilege of being alive. This is a vital part of the manipulation, for most of the families' bills are passed on to the people, who are not allowed, under penalty of law, to withdraw their financial support—try not paying your taxes!

In the wars the families fight among themselves, the common man acts as a cannon fodder. He has no control over events, neither is he asked his opinion. When did anyone ask if you wanted to pay for another bomb or not? This situation has not changed for five thousand years and that is OK; it is a part of our evolution. As Circle People, we have all come through childhood. In those formative years we were indoctrinated into the system and by the time we realized that we had been robbed of our power it was usually too late. We find it easier to acquiesce than to push against the tide of our inherited beliefs. So as Circle People, we "tick-tock" through life following orders like automatons. We pay for the governments that pass laws to restrict our activities. We sustain and pay for the law courts and the security forces that impose those laws. We work hard, at ridiculous rates of pay, to sustain the whole system and then a large portion of what we do get is grabbed back in taxes. The average small businessman in the United States, who owns a building as his place of business, pays a dozen different taxes. In addition, he has to pay to collect these taxes and other taxes for the government, without being reimbursed for his labor or expenses. The slavery laws that were passed last century were designed to protect the citizens from having to work for no pay. The government overlooks that. Then, with what is left after taxes, we have to support and feed our families and try to secure some kind of future for them. Who supports us? No one.

In America it was never meant to be like that. Thomas Jefferson was a metaphysician and he, with the Founding Fathers, wrote the Constitution of the United States on spiritual principles. Those good people would turn in their graves if they saw how the people were treated today. And because the United States has moved so far away from the freedom-loving ideas on which it was founded, it has begun to lose influence. Its share of the world market is cascading downwards and its ability to stand for goodness and love in the world falls away by the hour. The same has occurred in Britain. After the administration of Harold Wilson, which was one of the most manipulative in modern history, the country died. Now we witness a frantic clawing by the traditional institutions for whatever vestige of power remains to them. Meanwhile, millions of Britons are unemployed.

Once you realize what is going on and that, unfortunately, no one will ever support you, and that everything is designed to dis-empower you, then you can begin to get your power back. You will have a lot of fun doing it. But as you begin to affirm your power, be careful, for in trying to look after yourself you will be manipulated into believing that this is wrong. Do not fall for that. The system plays a subtle trick on the people, telling them that the "whole" is more important than the individual parts. This of course is ridiculous, for the whole is *only* the individual parts. What constitutes a country? Is it its geographic boundaries or its institutions or the land owners or the national football team? No, it is the millions of wonderful, individual people that make up its citizenry. Nothing else.

In perpetuating the idea that the individual is worthless, the system seeks to control. Those in power use the old tribal trick of linking their egocentric motivations to the will of God. So the people are maneuvered into thinking that the will of the hierarchies is the will of God. And because man cannot see God through his electro-magnetic curtain, he accepts that falsehood as truth. We are sold the idea that if we do not support the status quo or the nation that the families have carved out for themselves, then somehow we are going against the will of what God would want. The families exert influence and control over governments and they link the will of those governments to what they call the "national interest," which is no more than their interest. Then they maneuver the Circle People into thinking that they have to support that national interest even if the actions of the governments are not always righteous. Fear and guilt are the tools the manipulators use in the first place, rules and regulations follow that. Laws are entering the statute books at the rate of thousands per year.

Powerless to protest, the individual follows along, until the manipulation is so commonplace that he accepts it as natural. In fact he is hardly aware of any other possibility. You have fallen for it; I fell for it; we all have and that is perfect. You can't go past "tick-tock" without first having been immersed in it. In the less democratic societies, which include over eighty percent of the world, the manipulation is less subtle, for the rulers of those societies are more crude. Their methods of brute force and torture seem on the surface to be more bizarre, but they are no less infringing than what goes on in the societies that are supposedly democratic.

In an incredible stroke of utter brazenness, the system gets the Circle People to sustain, populate and support the very organizations that rob us of our power, thus tricking us into being our own jailers! And we wonder why things do not really change for the better.

This wonderful world, which God gave us so that we might learn about ourselves in it, is incredibly abundant. There is enough wealth, if divided equally among us, to make every man, woman and child on the planet a multi-millionaire. Yet we have famine and lack. Why? Because the system looks after itself, not the people. The powers-that-be hold onto their vested interests while the population is left to its own devices. They do the best they can to help each other, mailing bags of rice and so forth, but that will never fix the problem.

It seems almost impossible that things are on the verge of collapse, but they are. All you have to do is gently and lovingly take back your power and wait for the day when the intuitive people, those with love and caring in their hearts, those with a true spirituality, will inherit the earth.

But to get your power back you have to stand alone. You have to accept God as an energy source. By concentrating on the godliness within you and by accepting yourself as perfect (even if you are not), you gradually become more and more of the divine energy within. That energy is outside the Circle, so eventually your command is so great that you control every aspect of your life.

This is the first step, for if you see yourself as separate from God or the God Force, you drift back into the tribal ways. You are saying, "I am worthless, life is out of my hands, let the hierarchies, priests, or some outside force control." And the Universal Law, in its impartiality, responds by creating for you a reality that is somewhat spastic and full of uncertainty. The tail wags the dog and life controls you, not you, life.

With this attitude, affirmations become just mumblings—incantations to the hippopotamus god. But if you can truly believe that you are a part of the God Force, if you can view your life and the lives of others impartially, if you can allow everyone his or her own reality, without judging them, then gradually your energy becomes more and more infinite. As you do so, you step into another dimension of power, beyond the Circle, and you learn that you can bend reality to suit your ends. You will find that as you get results, spiritually you will grow a hundredfold.

The Universe is abundant.
Therefore I naturally feel abundant.
All my needs are met.

At your birth your subconscious mind began to record every feeling, every thought, every word that you spoke or was spoken to you. You accepted whatever your parents or teachers told you. Those who taught you probably loved you and did the best they could. But they had weakness and negativity within them and they taught that to you also. They taught you the tribal ways, they taught you the Circle limitation. They taught you fear and sin. They implied, through their weakness, that you would be unable to control your life. And so control became your struggle, not because you do not have the capacity within you, but because your great-great-grandmother felt weak and worthless, and she taught it to her family, and eventually your parents learned it and passed it on to you.

As a child, my mother taught me nursery rhymes. One that I always liked was "ring-a-ring of roses." It was fun and we all enjoyed falling to the floor on the last line. My subconscious mind accepted that nursery rhyme as being good. I performed it because it made my mother happy. But let us look at it for a moment. In its English version it goes like this:

Ring-a-ring of roses,

A pocket full of posies,

Atishoo, atishoo,

We all fall down.

This old English nursery rhyme was written at the time of the great plague. The "ring of roses" was a skin blemish that appeared under the armpit of those who contracted the disease. People believed that the disease was circulated in the foul air of the cities and so they carried with them a bunch of sweet-smelling flowers, or "posies," to protect themselves from infection. "Atishoo, atishoo," was a sign that the fever had gripped its victim. And "we all fall down," of course, meant that no one survived.

Cheerful stuff. I was taught that at the tender age of three and so, probably, were you. And we all danced to the joys of the plague and the fun of dying a grisly death. We did not know any better, and the people who taught us and loved us knew no better either. Our subconscious minds accepted "atishoo, atishoo, we all fall down," as real. Now, it is unlikely that you will contract the bubonic plague. But every time you sneeze your mind brings forth "fall down, fall down," and your energy drops. It must. That is what the subconscious mind believes is real. Unless you tell it something different.

You are made up of billions and billions of beliefs. Beliefs about your body, beliefs about your intellectual worth, beliefs about how attractive you are. Beliefs about God, sin, life after death, morality, beliefs about the tribe or society you live in, beliefs about your family and what should or should not be done and so on.

All of these beliefs came from somewhere. Or you developed them by finding out what others believed and you accepted bits and pieces to suit yourself. These beliefs are your reality. They are truth to you, and your mind holds onto them with grim determination. Yet if you look at what you do believe, you will find that much of it has little or no foundation. Instead of serving you, your beliefs hold you back. Much of it is just tribal hogwash, energy that has been handed down from one inadequate generation to the next. And you accepted it.

Spiritually, these beliefs are a part of your evolution and in a way they are good because they allow you to step beyond them. By dealing with weakness, bit by bit, you begin to believe in yourself. And so when the tribe says to you, "Throw two oranges into the river to appease the hippopotamus god or the crops will not grow," you have the courage to say, "Baloney." And you go out and buy a bag of fertilizer instead.

Spiritual growth basically means going beyond mass thinking, to a point where you have so much confidence in your reality that you know you can stand alone. In the process you discover that you are the Living Spirit within—eternal, immortal and infinite—that in fact you are limitless.

Recently a lady called me from Abiline, Texas. She had plenty of troubles, body problems, emotional problems, interpersonal problems. She was out of work and living on government food stamps. I asked her why she felt she had so many problems. She replied she was going through her "troubled years." I asked her why she believed she had to go through bad years. She replied that her astrologer had told her that her planetary configuration was adverse and that these would be troubled times. I was curious to know who her astrologer was. She explained that it was a lady she had met casually on a bus. So we took a look at the situation. Here was a lady from Abiline, Texas, who sounded pretty neat but she had problems. The reason she had problems was because one day, being totally out of tune, she bumped into a lady on a bus who in hoping to help her, told her that things were going to be bad. Her mind believed it. And bit by bit the reality she experienced reflected her beliefs. Things literally fell apart.

I said to the lady, "What if I tell you that you are just plain wrong, that in fact this is going to be a very good year for you, that things will turn around and that your body will be totally healed within thirty days." She would not accept that. She told me I was nuts and rang off!

Whatever you believe is either ugly or beautiful, helpful or hindering. You wear it like a coat. It affects what you are. Your beliefs show up in your life as failure or success. As children we learn that life is hard and that we have to struggle, so as adults we put out into the Universal Law, "Give me struggle." It responds, "What kind of struggle do you want?" "Well, how's about constant struggle," we reply. The shelf falls off the kitchen wall and brains the cat, the car won't start, and an astral voice from the phone company informs us the phone is just about to be cut off and we think, perfect, I am struggling like crazy and its only 9:15 a.m.. Difficulty becomes a natural part of what we project.

You may not be aware of it but people perceive minute details about you even on a first meeting. If you go to a job interview and you have just been told that you are living through your troubled years, you project that and the interviewer may pick up a lack of confidence. If for example, you have just been fighting with your neighbor, that negative energy might appear as fragmentation and the interviewer might translate it as a lack of cohesiveness. It is important therefore to be aware of what it is you project and to be sure that you do not project negativity.

You may not be aware that most of the energy you reflect into the Universal Law comes from within. Usually you are not aware that you are projecting energy in such a way because it is a part of the vast reservoirs of information in your unconscious. You may consciously feel that you are a very positive person but from deep within you do not project the same strength, and so you constantly find that life does not seem to go the way you want it to. To resolve this, you have to look carefully at what it is that the *inner you* actually believes. This is achieved through *introspection, dedication,* and *sanctuary*. These techniques are discussed in later chapters.

To come to a life full of power you must gradually displace inner weakness by concentrating on your positive strengths. Affirmations are a way for you to begin that change. Let me give you an example. One of my partners in Europe found a certain tribe of people extremely irritating. He did not like their tribal customs, nor the way they handled their financial affairs. He felt their restaurants were revolting and he saw the people as limited and negative. In addition, he was angry that his situation forced him to work with them. Each time he met one, or saw one in the street, my partner would bring up all the negativity that he felt. That hindered him.

I suggested he reprogram his mind by affirming ten things that were good about these people. He found that to be a challenge, but in the end his list ran something like this: "The tribe is very creative, many world-class musicians come from this tribe, * tribe is very family-oriented, the tribe has a good sense of humor (even though he had trouble understanding it), the tribe is often very philanthropic," and so on and so forth.

Over a period of a year he completely changed what his subconscious mind felt about these people. He became more relaxed and he found that he began to draw to him a better quality of person from within that tribe, because his *inner self* reflected their positive strengths, not their weaknesses.

Using this exercise you can overcome almost any negative energy pattern, given determination and time. The mind is strong, and has most likely been in a dominant position for many years. As you begin to affirm and work on controlling your life, the mind of course will react. Often, when people become sick and begin to work on healing themselves, they actually get sicker before they get better. This is because the mind knows that when your body is out of balance, it can control and dominate you, so it has a vested interest in keeping you unbalanced.

The path of power is basically a tussle between inner objectives: the mind pulling you back, and you, through determination and courage, heading constantly outwards. As you journey within yourself, facing the programming that has accumulated there, the task will seem endless. But as you clear away the debris, more energy will surround you. The clearer you become, the more the Force becomes a part of your life. Eventually, you will reach a clarity whereby whatever you concentrate on, knowing it to be granted, will become real.

As you work with the mind, you repeat your affirmations over and over again and eventually the mind accepts those affirmations as real and a new energy replaces the old weaknesses.

As a student on the Path I learned that every time a person has eye contact with you, or touches you, there is an energy transference. This leaves you open to receive energy. Sometimes, what you receive is not much fun. The world is often negative and scared. You do not need that. Knowing this, I trained my mind to say the word "peace" silently whenever I came into contact with strangers in public places. At first, I had to remember to say the word each time, and of course, I often forgot. But over the years this habit has become so much a part of my life that now my mind comes forward with the word "peace" automatically. It has a cause of its own, so to speak.

By wishing a million people "peace" then a million more, you create that energy within you, and gradually what you create is a peaceful world around you. The affirmation becomes real by its constant repetition and by the fact that you really mean it. If you say "I am power" ten times a day for ten years, you *become* it.

There is nothing you cannot go beyond. But sometimes the effort is great and the weakness so prevalent, that negativity overwhelms us. You have to take to the Path as if your life depended on it, for in a way it does. Whenever an uncomfortable situation arises, it is often the mind reacting. This is the very moment that you need to push through. So if handling your body is a drag, that is probably the very thing that you have been avoiding. By facing the uncomfortable areas in your life, you grow spiritually — through learning about yourself.

Unconscious people stuff down the uncomfortable bits and paper over their feelings with drugs and alcohol. Eventually the inner areas of turmoil filter to the surface and manifest as serious disease or traumatic events. By having the courage to face yourself, you transcend what has gone before and you come into a different alignment. Think of it like this: you enter this plane and you are taught the basics of the Circle philosophy. You accept negativity and weakness along with strengths and know-how. By the time you are a teenager most of the foundation had been laid. Your spiritual challenge, then, is to practice controlling the energy you have and gradually to discard the bits you do not like . Sound like a neat assignment? It is. And you have the rest of your life to complete the project.

You see, just getting through life is not enough. If you have any kind of real goal you will want to challenge yourself. People find a little rut to follow and they stick to it. This is because the mind does not like spontaneity or change. People tend to create patterns they are comfortable with and they pursue that path day-in and day-out. Everything is fine for twenty-seven years, and then one day there is a bear on the path and it eats them.

Not only have they not lived, but they have also not listened to their inner feelings that said, "Hey wait a minute, there is something wrong with the pattern today." The point is not how long you live, it is the quality and variety of the life you live. The purpose of being in the world is to experience it. If you spend the whole of your life doing exactly the same thing each and every day, time flies, and soon old age creeps up and bites you on the bum, before you have had a chance to really experience things.

The energy of affirmation is in saying, "I am moving up. There is no limit to what I can experience. I am going to live life. Any opportunity I find to experience something new I will take, given the wherewithall. I will canoe the Amazon; I will parachute from an aircraft. I will visit every major art gallery in the world. I will write three books—and sell them—I will sing at Carnegie Hall. I will visit fifty countries. I will heal my body. That will take me through to Tuesday. Then I will visit the pyramids, fall in love with a fantastic person, make a pot of money, fly the Grand Canyon, visit Tibet and learn to levitate. Sunday, I will have a little nap and wash my clothes, since on Monday I am off to Kenya on safari."

Everything is out there waiting for you. All you have to do is walk up and declare yourself in. No need for permission. You just need the courage to say, "Include me." Providing you have the energy to pull it off you can do what you like. And the Universal Law, being impartial, will be only too delighted to deliver.

As you work with your power, you will be amazed at the

way doors will open for you. People will feel your heightened energy and they will want to be with you—they will actually seek you out. You will find yourself included more and more. As things open up for you, paths you never knew existed will appear before you. You will be able to affirm, "I am power," from a position of strength. You will say, "Opportunity finds me," and your mind will believe it, because it will experience these magically spontaneous happenings. It will not be make-believe any more. You will be there. On the top of the Great Pyramid at dawn, overlooking the Nile valley. Ahead of you will lie an eternal future.

Courage is a natural part of my being. By facing life I transcend it.

3
WHAT DO YOU REALLY WANT?

You must have heard the story of the prisoner who finally finished his long prison sentence. Once he was released from prison he felt lost. He could not handle being in the outside world. So he committed an insignificant crime in order to get sent back to prison where he felt safe, and where his life was organized for him. The mind behaves like the prisoner. It likes restriction and limitation because that is what it is used to. Limitation allows one not to have to face oneself. It allows you to stay put.

Once, on an inner journey, I was joined by a celestial being. I could not see him but I could feel his presence. He was a teacher. He said he would show me the limitless nature of infinity. Somehow, he moved me over a great distance. In a flash, I found myself standing in the middle of nowhere. Infinity stretched out around me. The experience was very unusual. I had never realized that infinity had a particular "feeling." But it did.

The infinite distance in front of me was comfortable; much like thinking about the future. The infinity behind me was harder to deal with. We are used to a past that is structured, solid and unchanging. But in the dimension in which I found myself with this inner being, the past gradually changed. It had a type of emotion which rose or fell according to what people felt about it.

The infinite distance above me was no more than just interesting. It reminded me of the night sky and many a crick in the neck when pondering a distant twinkle, wondering who the hell is up there. Then I looked down and freaked out! The infinite distance below me was very disconcerting. As humans, we are used to looking down at the sight of reassuring bedrock. *Terra-firma*— the more firmer the less terror! Imagine looking down past your feet to an infinite distance below. You cannot help feeling that you are about to fall. And yet, poised as I was, with this invisible being at my side, I somehow stayed up. I had a glimpse of total freedom. It was as if a heavy mantle slipped momentarily from my shoulders and I realized that we are all free, if only we can wake to that fact.

The being told me that I could move in any direction I wished. Great fear wafted through me. I was unable to move. I was like the prisoner unable to capitalize on his freedom. An opportunity missed perhaps, and yet I had learned. I realized that any restriction we feel as humans is just illusion. There is no such thing as "can't." There is no limit. Words are inadequate to describe the immense possibilities that lie before you. The world, even the universe is at your feet. But you have to go at it as if your life depended on it. You have to be clear what it is you want.

Imagine a high spiritual being appearing to you and saying, "You can have anything you want. Anything." What would you ask for? Would you be open and ready to receive? Would you know that the things you choose were spiritually advantageous, or would you choose things that fuel the ego and perhaps set you back?

Most people in the world have no clue as to where they are going. They do not know what they want. They have no real idea of how to express themselves or develop their creativity, so they drift endlessly. Why? Because if you put into the Universal Law, I don't know what I want, it responds, "If you don't know, mate, why should we?" So if you have no plans for your life, you are in the boat and the rudder is on the pier.

On one of my first journeys in the light, I was amazed to find that the light is not emotionally involved in our lives. This was a shock, as I had been brought up to believe that God somehow cared about what I was doing day-to-day and that decisions were being made for me somewhere, someplace. I now know that this is not so. The light does not have a volition for you. In a way this is good, for it grants you absolute freedom. But it is vital for you to know what you want. It is no good saying, "I want something better than this. My life is the pits. God, send me down a pot of money and get me out of here." That will not work. It is much too vague, and energy would have difficulty finding you.

Think about what you want. Write down the ten things you want more than anything else. Imagine yourself having them. Create a battle plan that delineates your path to the goal. Avoid all irrelevant side tracks.

Let me give you an example. Let us say you want to be a great musician, and you want your music to create great wealth for you. But you are frustrated in making it work, so you get drunk from time to time. You cannot communicate with an inner energy if you do not maintain balance, if you get drunk all of the time. Drinking becomes an irrelevant side path, so dump it.

Get rid of everything that holds you back. "But I have to carry this eight-foot grandfather clock strapped to my wrist because it has been in my family for three hundred years. People will think ill of me if I do not maintain the heritage." Two virgins off a cliff!

The main difficulty people have is in clarifying what they want and in realizing they are free to get it. If you track your day in minute detail and watch your results, you will find that most of the effort you put in brings no reward and little satisfaction. Often it is just twenty to twenty-five percent of your concentrated effort that actually brings results. We waste time, we hang out with the wrong people, we travel to the wrong places. We dither and dally, waiting for someone to give us permission to succeed. No one will ever give permission and no one will ever thank you.

In modern society, there is still a fear of success. Success takes you away from the people you grew up with. It has a way of showing them up. And so we tend not to want to do well in case we upset a loved one.

While travelling in Canada, I met a young lawyer. In talking to her, I discovered that she was constantly making silly mistakes at work. She was very bright and very capable; her inaccuracy was inconsistent with her capabilities. She was married to another lawyer. You may have already guessed the reason for her poor performance: her husband was mediocre. I met him once, full of piss and wind and not much talent. But she was worried that her marriage would fall apart. Her *inner self* created situations in which she looked bad, so that she did not surpass her husband. I told her to tell him how she felt, and suggested she form her own practice. I often wondered what happened. Did she continue to perform less than her best, or did she step to the Path of Power?

I feel good, therefore my life is good.

Getting clear about what it is you want is the first step in materializing your goals. Once you know what it is you want, you will move ahead, as if the Universe has already granted your wish. As you do that, the energy begins to build. It begins to shape itself from your feelings and thoughts, and eventually the power is so strong that the energy moves from strong fantasy to reality.

4
DEDICATION: THE WARRIOR'S PRAYER TO HIMSELF

It is rare that you meet a person who is truly dedicated. When you do, you find that he is almost always very successful. Dedication is the warrior's prayer to him or herself. It is a mode of fierce concentration. One becomes so attached and devoted to the cause that eventually one's desires materialize. The world is full of obstacles. If you review the lives of the great men and women who have walked the earth plane, you will find it was dedication that made them special. They persevered despite the odds. They achieved their goals through thick and thin. They overcame social, physical, and financial difficulties and created success.

Dedication is vital. You have to live your life like a warrior and breathe your ambitions. If you are half-hearted the Universal Law responds spastically. If you lack courage, the energy around you lacks courage. If you falter, the Universal Law falters with you. If, for example, you want to be an actress, you have to get in the program. You have to train, go to auditions, be a part of the industry. There is no point in living in a field in the middle of nowhere and saying, "I am a great actress and the only reason I am not on Broadway is because I prefer this muddy field."

The Universal Law will give you anything you want, but it cannot deliver it to you like a package service. You have to be in the market place. And you have to be ready to take advantage of a situation as it arises. Perseverence allows you to hold on while the Universal Law delivers. Many allow themselves to be bumped off course by setbacks. If you have to wash dishes for five years to become a great actress, then be prepared to wash dishes for six just in case. *That* is dedication.

When I was a teenager, I had a friend who played field hockey. He was not very fast or even very agile, yet somehow he played right wing, a position that calls for great speed in hurtling up and down the outside edge of the field. What was special about this guy was that even though he was not really built for the task, he had great tenacity. Whenever he tackled the opposition for the ball, he never quit. He would harry opponents mercilessly. And even when he got beat for speed he would double back and harry the next guy. This little winger had a dedication that was almost perverse. He was also incredibly crafty. When he had the ball he had a way of running that put others off balance. The ball stayed stuck to his stick like epoxy. He played with moves that no one had ever seen before. This winger would run and run, and would often beat others faster than himself because he never gave in. He was the leading goal scorer and an inspiration to his team. He was selected for training camp by the English national team and eventually became one of the best wingers in the land. He did it by transcending his lack of speed through dedication, tenacity and craftiness.

How crafty are you? Can you go past limitations? Can you still be there once the others have quit? If you can, your success is assured, for the Universal Law will respond.

Having dedication is saying, "I am the power within. There is nothing I cannot do. There is no one to stand in my way. I am free and I will never quit. If it takes me forty years, I will be there. Carnegie Hall, the Royal Opera House—whatever. The fact that I cannot sing a note and that I sound like a frog in a bag is just an illusion. I will take lessons. I will be the greatest ninety-four year-old opera singer in the world, even if I have to live to be a hundred to achieve it!"

The way to develop dedication is to begin to become fiercely dedicated to yourself. This means concentrating on your needs, concentrating on those projects that give you pleasure and taking time to acknowledge that you are here on the earth plane to develop your evolution, not to develop something else. Once you allow yourself that level of self-nurturing attention, then life gradually takes on new meaning, and you become able to create a dedication to yourself, your family, or to those causes you feel strongly about.

Once you have dedication, you have in your pocket a great tool. Its very consistency will make you stand out in a crowd. It is not a flash in the pan but a gradual energy built bit by bit, year in, year out. Until one day you are at the top looking down. Recently I watched a singer being interviewed on TV. The singer had had three smash hits in less than a year and he was asked how he felt about the acclaim he had received. Jokingly he replied, "I am going to write a book called: 'How to Be an Overnight Success in Seventeen Years,' " for it had taken that long for him to compose his first big hit.

Many quit just before they hit the jackpot. Then they complain that the Universal Law does not provide for them, which is a bunch of rubbish. If you don't have what you want, it means that you are still on the journey. You might be close to the goal, yet being close to the best restaurant in town is not dinner. You have to press on to that final glorious conclusion.

Eight years ago, I was with a group of about forty guys who took a bet that we could dig a hole the size of a large house in two days, using no mechanical equipment. The hole was to be forty feet deep and about sixty feet wide. That is a lot of earth to push. With picks and shovels we began to dig. Wheelbarrow after wheelbarrow was hauled to the surface from the bottom of the hole. After about ten hours night fell, so we rigged up some makeshift lights and continued to dig through the night. Around four in the morning it began to rain. The hole became a muddy pit. The effort in getting just one wheelbarrow to the top of the hole was excruciating. Our bones were frozen and our progress was slowed to a crawl. It seemed we were beaten.

We could have quit, and people would still have praised us for trying hard, but we would have lost, and we knew it. Then one of the men found some rope and we divided into two-man teams. One had the rope around his waist in mulelike fashion, the other pushed the barrow. Using this method we could haul the barrowloads of mud to the top. We worked through to dawn and even though the milky sun of the new day warmed our spirits somewhat, the task still seemed impossible. Pressing on, we worked without sleep. We transcended pain and fatigue and found a second wind from deep within us. At the end of the day the rain stopped and we dug through the wet earth to the more manageable dry earth below. We continued to use the mule system since we found it faster to have one digger and one hauler, each encouraging the other.

The coordination was symphonic: forty men, coming and going, swinging picks in a confined space, each acutely aware of the other, each supporting the other, all driven by a dedication to complete the job.

After forty-four hours of non-stop digging we found ourselves short of the target. So we began to run. We hauled the barrows at a trot, we ran from one side of the hole to the next, we took no breaks, we dug faster and faster. And as we sped up, the excitement energized us to push through our pain thresholds and to dig faster still. The hole was finished to the exact dimensions after forty-seven hours and forty-three minutes. We finished the impossible with seventeen minutes to spare! No one got paid. It was done for honor. A month later a mechanical digger filled the hole back in again. Dedication: the stuff of life.

I dedicate my life to the power within me. Through dedication I unfold naturally to the highest potential of my being.

5
AFFIRMATIONS OF WORD

As was said earlier, there are four types of affirmations: affirmations of word, thought, feeling, and of essence or action. Let us discuss each of them. And let us look at how to wrap them into a "battle plan" for life.

Affirmations of word are the closest thing to prayer. But instead of praying to a God outside of yourself, you pray to yourself, who is God. You say, "I am the power, I am the light, I control my life." An affirmation of word is almost like a mantra. It does not really matter if what you are affirming is not totally true as yet. By repeating an affirmation over and over again, it becomes embedded in the subconscious mind, and eventually becomes your reality.

An affirmation of word will serve for almost anything—health, wealth, happiness—whatever you are concentrating on at the time. The affirmations you compose personally are the strongest, for they reflect what your mind actually feels. I can give you examples of affirmations, but you should change them to suit your own feelings. The culture in which I was brought up has power words but they will not necessarily be your power words.

When I was about eight years old I contracted malaria in Africa which for a while threatened my life. My fever reached 106 degrees. For a small boy that is extremely hot! On the third day of the fever my mother told me that she was going to pull together a special healing energy on my behalf. She came to my room in the early evening, and holding my hand, began to recite in Latin the following invocation:

Behold the cross of God.

Negative influences, be gone.

The lion of the tribe of Judah

is victorious.

David rules, David rules.

Allelujah, Allelujah.

She repeated this invocation for hours on end. I fell asleep and by next morning my fever had broken. The Latin words were just jibberish, but to her they had power. Using that power she created within herself a healing influence and projected it to me. Her message worked.

It is important that an affirmation have emotional force behind it and that it means something to you. Emotion harnesses the energy. It puts you in flow. If you just mumble prayers you do not have the same power you have if there is something about the prayer that you feel strongly about. The words do not really matter: it is your feelings that count.

At my school we had to do a lot of praying and we were often bored. So we would make up our own words to the prayers to amuse ourselves, mumbling them quietly under our breath. In the Lord's Prayer we substituted the names of London suburbs for the key words. The prayer went like this: "Our Farnham, who art in Hendon, Harrow be thy name, thy Kingston come, thy Wimbledon, in Esher as it is in Harringay..." You get the idea.

Before long, I could not say the Lord's Prayer in its correct fashion. Even today, the words, "Our Farnham, who art in Hendon, Harrow be thy name..." are power words to me. At the age of ten they represented my rebellion. I was saying, "I am what I am; I am an individual. If God does not have a sense of humor, tough."

And so as you set up affirmations for your day, be sure your words really mean something, instead of using other words which may not have the same impact. They may have connotations that do not really support your position as an individual in control of his or her own destiny.

It is important that you set up some kind of sanctuary in your life, that allows you to pull out of the Circle mind set and have peace and quiet to work upon your affirmation of self. Your sanctuary may be a room in the house or perhaps a walk at dawn. By setting up times to be alone with yourself, you allow additional power to flow.

If you can, try to develop a regimen whereby you dedicate the same time each day to your inner growth, so that a rhythm develops. The in-breathing and out-breathing of the Universal Mind flows in consort with your intentions. You will be amazed at the expansion of your perceptions. I recommend twenty-four minutes for the process, one for each hour of the day.

During this sanctuary time you will decide on your affirmation for the day. Here are a few that I like:

Dawn Affirmations

I AM ETERNAL, IMMORTAL, UNIVERSAL AND INFINITE.

MY EXPECTATIONS ARE TRULY LIMITLESS.

I AM WHAT I AM, AND WHAT I AM HAS BEAUTY AND STRENGTH.

MAY THE FRESHNESS OF THIS NEW DAY VITALIZE AND HEAL MY BODY. MAY THERE BE BALANCE AND POWER IN THIS DAY.

THE BEAUTY THAT I SEE IS A PART OF ALL THINGS, FOR I AM TRULY A PART OF ALL THINGS.

IN THIS DAY I EXPRESS LOVE TO EACH PERSON I MEET, FOR I KNOW THAT I AM TRULY LOVABLE.

THE UNIVERSE IS ABUNDANT, THEREFORE I FEEL ABUN – DANT. ALL MY NEEDS ARE MET.

MAY THE BEAUTY OF THIS DAY UNFOLD STRONGLY. MAY THE CREATIVITY WITHIN ME MANIFEST TO ITS HIGHEST POSSIBILITY.

Dawn is your strongest hour for expressing affirmations. As you wake refreshed from the night you can place into your consciousness thoughts and feelings that will mold your day to suit your highest evolution. You have a blank slate on which to write, relatively free of negative emotion. In addition, if you rise at dawn or even before dawn, the rest of the world has not begun to influence the Universal Law, so your affirmations have more force.

Take a few moments to consider your day. Visualize events flowing, see people accepting your ideas and your energy, feel in control of what is moving toward you. Feel the magic that is a natural part of life. If you are faced with a difficult situation, take a moment to breathe in, visualizing that situation and as you exhale, project light and love to that person or situation and see it, or them, reacting positively to your energy. In this way you develop a line of strength and power that you feed into the Universal Law.

This simple procedure acts as a guideline that prohibits intrusion of adverse feelings into the unfolding patterns. Of course, there is always the possibility that your own defenses will break down or that something negative may penetrate the parabolas of energy you have set up, but that is rare. If you maintain balance through the day you will find there is always light on the path, that your charm is infused into the day, and that your highest evolution is assured.

By taking a few moments before dawn or when you rise, you affirm that you are a conscious, creative being. Your energy has risen in order to better manipulate your destiny, materialize desires and control events. If you set aside twenty-four minutes, one for each hour of the day, to allow your inner guidance to project out into your life, you affirm that your seat of power lies within. And as you move through the day with that intention or alignment, you are saying, "I know that I exist in the physical world, but I control from within."

The twenty-four minutes can be a meditation or just a period of silent introspection. Perhaps you can walk out of doors, listen to some special music or be near the sea or some expanse of water. The main point is that you meditate every day and that you establish a rhythm so that your twenty-four minutes is at approximately the same time each day. This allows the inner worlds to communicate with you. Gradually you will develop a power that surpasses buffeting emotions and worry.

Having once set up your day, it is important to maintain the energy. Any negative emotion or negative conflict will destroy your energy, and the power of your affirmations will dissipate. So pick a few affirmations and repeat them to yourself from time to time. It can be one word: strength, love—whatever you want. Then, as the day proceeds, the energy you carry with you will protect you, and keep you from trouble.

During the middle of the day, take a few moments to be with yourself. It's hard, for there are always things to do. And yet a moment invested in energy will save you endless time otherwise spent rushing around trying, forcing, and struggling. Life is not meant to be a struggle; just a gentle progression from one point to another, much like walking through a valley on a sunny day.

As you begin to see your life as a manifestation of energy, you will find that your best work is in "consciousness." This means that as you think and feel and indicate what it is you want in thought, reality is transformed around you. Eventually you will perceive only dimensions of your own creation and these thought forms will have beauty.

An energy booster in the middle of the day is important. But do not make it an onerous chore. If you end up crossed-legged on the filing cabinet in the typing pool, chanting your OMs, that is too much. Just pull to one side in consciousness and be with yourself. Look at the day and feel how strongly it has gone, feel how the spontaneity of events has treated you, link or anchor the positive events to your inner feelings, see how you created the wellness of the day. This is done by reliving the events in your thought and saying, "I created that, I did it well, I have the wherewithall, I know what I am doing, I feel in control." By reviewing the successes, however slight, and making them a part of your consciousness, you set up and affirm that the rest of the day will go well. You place one more stick on the fire, so to speak, and you anchor or link the positive to the eternity within you.

Your successes may be small but it is important to look at them. In doing so you develop personal triumphs. It can be just arriving at work on time, completing a project, interacting with your children in a loving way, meeting with a friend and so forth. Often as humans we tend to see our lives as insignificant. They are not. Everything means something. Each task is a part of your heroic quest for transcendance. If you take time to honor your successes you will experience power in a world where most do not.

As you take this short break in the middle of the day, I want you to try to re-link yourself with nature, and remember the sanctuary that you created at dawn. If you cannot actually walk in nature, at least take a moment to look out of the window at the trees, at the sky, to feel that eternity within you. As you do so, the physical plane becomes smaller and the infinity within you expands. Say, again, "I am a part of all things, eternal, immortal, universal, and infinite. My expectations are truly limitless."

If you can get out into the woods or to a park, take a moment to actually touch nature, with your feelings, with your thought, with your body. Stand by a tree, touch it, draw from its power and feel the non-judgmental life-force that courses through the tree and flows to you. Visualize it flowing through your body, washing away tiredness and negativity, refreshing you. Take a moment to look at part of nature in minute detail. Pause to look inside a flower. Just stare at it for ten seconds and see if you can feel the dimensions of existence that are going on inside. Try to feel your connection with that universe. It will help you pull out of the emotion and mentality of the Circle and into a dimension of pure God Force. If you cannot find a flower, find something else. It can be just a rock. Go into the rock and, with your feelings, experience the silence, feel how the rock expresses eternity, and feel yourself aligning with it. By touching infinity through nature you allow the inner, *spiritual* you to rejuvenate. When it is refreshed you dominate reality around you.

This day continues well.
I feel successful. I feel strong.
There is beauty in all things.

Take this moment to boost the energy of your body. Your ability to express yourself in the day will be closely linked to your physical strength. It is hard for you to be positive and strong if your body will not respond accordingly. Since you exist in the physical plane, its considerations are paramount.

If your midday affirmation includes a moment of resting and rejuvenation, the words you utter are enhanced by an actual upsurge of physical vitality. See each part of your body respond with strength, notice the light infusing each and every molecule of your being, see yourself grow in power, watch how you control the measures of time in which you work. See everything flowing. Be sure that your food intake at midday is not so heavy that your energy is wiped out, especially if you have projects to complete. Understand that as soon as you take in alcohol or large amounts of carbohydrates and protein your body basically stops. It has to, in order to digest, which reduces your energy immediately. If you have an important appointment and you are going to need all of your power for it, do not schedule it right after a meal. Your ability to affect reality is diminished.

There are certain times in the week that are much stronger than others. For example, you would never make an appointment with a bank on a Friday to discuss financing for a new project and never *ever* after Friday lunchtime. No matter how good your plan is, the man you talk to will have "gone fishing" in his consciousness, even if he is nodding politely from time to time. Your plan cannot have impact on him.

The first few hours of Monday morning are also a poor choice. People spend the weekend thinking about all the things they have to do in the office Monday. When they arrive, they need the first few hours to settle down and to establish control over their affairs. If you arrive too early you infringe on their time and they will not be as open. Indeed your presence may irritate them.

Obviously, every situation is different, but generally Tuesday, Wednesday or Thursday mornings are the best times for introducing new ideas or for presenting yourself for an interview. Midweek afternoons are strong for those occasions when you have a plan to get across and there is going to be some resistance. You should go in having had nothing to eat and try to make sure the people you are dealing with have had a substantial lunch. One way to ensure this is to take them out yourself. Stuff 'em silly. You nibble a cracker. The best negotiator I ever met just drank water. I never once saw him eat during the day. He would take you to lunch, buy you anything you desired—he would only drink water. I noticed that he got what he wanted in life.

If you can be disciplined and control your energy during the day, you will find that you have more time to yourself. Getting through the day will not dissipate your energy and when, eventually, you have more time to yourself, that time can be more creatively spent and you will have the reserves you need. Taking those few moments for affirmation and introspection allows you time to regenerate your inner energy as well as your physical strength.

Here are some midday affirmations:

THIS DAY CONTINUES WELL; I FEEL SUCCESSFUL, I FEEL STRONG. THERE IS BEAUTY IN ALL THINGS.

MY STAMINA IS STRONG; PEOPLE RESPOND TO MY ENERGY. I FEEL CREATIVE, I FEEL LOVE, BECAUSE I LOVE AND RESPECT MYSELF.

I EXERCISE ABSOLUTE CONTROL OVER MY TIME. I FEEL DIRECTED, I FEEL ORGANIZED, AND SO I PULL BALANCE AND ORDER TO ME AT ALL TIMES.

MY CREATIVITY FLOWS FROM WITHIN ME. I PULL TO ME ALL THAT I WILL EVER NEED.

6
YOUR WORD AS LAW

The idea of your word as law is discussed briefly in my book *The Force*, but let us review the concept in detail as it applies to affirmations.

First you must understand how self-image is created. At birth the mind begins to record each and every event of your life. Nothing is ever lost from that record. Events sometimes become less intense with the passage of time, but they are still there in your subconscious as a part of your reality and can be recalled through hypnosis. During the first eighteen months of your life you spent much of the time asleep or at deep levels of mind and brain wave activity. During those times you soaked up the atmosphere, and even though your mind did not understand intellectually what was being said the "feeling" behind the words spoken by those around you entered your mind and settled in your subconscious.

This created a base for your behavior and experience and introduced you to the energy of the Circle. As you began to learn language, you began to understand how to control your environment. You could say, "Mummy, give me an ice cream," and you could get what you wanted, especially if your demand was made with enough emotion or at the right place and time. Your mind learned a format for materializing its desires. The format included timing and emotion. It knew that a request for an ice cream spoken at a whisper at three in the morning was not as effective as say the same request screamed at one hundred and twenty decibels in the center of the supermarket, coupled with your knocking all the cans off the shelf in a ceremonious clatter, to the intense embarrassment of your poor mother.

As you grew, you learned more techniques of self-realization. At the age of three or four you began to develop the rudiments of intellect, which empowered you even further. You could conceptualize the future. You would say "Dad, are we going to the beach tomorrow?" and, in doing so, you could make sure your needs would be actualized.

However, as you grew older and as your charm as a child dissipated, you discovered that your ability to affect the reality around you was limited. You would make a request of your parents and it would be denied. You would attempt to expand your physical environment by, say, walking up the street and your mother would haul you back. And so you began to program the mind with limitations and restriction. There were things that you could do and could not do. Often there was neither rhyme nor reason to explain your success or failure. It followed the whims of those looking after you. Because of this an element of uncertainty developed in your life.

Your ability to materialize events was greatly restricted. To combat this a child lives in his or her own fantasies. This enables him or her to feel powerful and to develop self-image. Remember that the child is not really a child but an infinite Higher Self in a small body. Because it is not possible for a female to gestate a grown human, childhood is a necessary part of our dimension. Even though it is fraught with complications and difficulties, it allows the Higher Self a sheltered start. It gives you time to reconcile and accept your presence in the physical plane. This can take a while. Many people report a sense of great awe and sadness in childhood as they come to the realization that they are stuck in the physical. Often a child will talk of other beings in other dimensions and this, I believe, is a part of its initial recall, a part of its inner knowing. You come to accept the fact that you are in the physical plane, but there is also a sense of sadness, of having left your abode of light in order to be here.

Fantasy, therefore, is the mind's way of reconciling its inability to totally experience or control its environment. Your parents contributed to this ineffectual feeling by allowing you only so much scope. As you tried to expand or as you tried to develop self-image or self-realization you were often stymied in your attempts, partly because your tender age was a danger to you and partly because (and this might sound strange) your parents knew instinctively that you, a child, held a power that they had lost, that your strength was metaphysically greater than theirs. All parents know this on an inner level and, to combat what is basically a threat to the parent's self-image, they restrict the child further than is really necessary for its safety.

By the time a person is old enough to become a parent, he or she has developed a mind set that comes out of life experience. It is very hard for a mother to accept that the babe in her arms is actually more in tune and protected than she. So what happens is that her experience of life, and the mind set she has created through experience, is superimposed on the child, cramping its development. This cramping is an accepted part of being in the physical and I believe that it is forseen by the Higher Self. The imposition of your parents' experiential patterns, beliefs and attitudes locks you into a dimension of consciousness with all the accoutrements of limitation and restrictions that follow.

There are created within the mind, lines of communication, linkages that form rigid patterns. The child will conceive an idea and, instead of being free-reigning and fluid, it follows the line or linkage laid as a part of its foundation. The fantasy aspect of a child's existence is its frantic attempt to cross over or to circumvent those linkages and to hold a pattern of consciousness that is individual. But this struggle is short-lived and often the fantasy period is only endorsed by the parents for a short while. Sooner or later they will want you to get serious, settle down, and study the "mind blocks" and foundations that they feel appropriate.

As a child you would put a paper bag on your head and you would say, "I am the big chief of the Uli-Guli tribe" and your Dad would say, "Stop messing about and get in the car." So the mind began to experience an ineffectual weakness. When you said something, more often than not it would be banged down or ignored. You would not experience your word as law.

In fact every one else seemed to have control over you, even total strangers. As your psyche or *inner self* faced these reversals of its fantasy patterns, it had to reconcile its upset. It came to a gradual acceptance that it did not have the ability to create its absolute reality, and so it began to downgrade its aspirations, words, and thought forms as unimportant and not real.

Perhaps you might make a claim such as, "I can be a great violinist," but when challenged you back down and say that you were only joking. But of course you were not. You do have that feeling within you, it is just that the thought form has difficulty having integrity or self-worth. It feels that what others think is more important than what you think. Interesting is it not, that the mind will believe a total stranger, who perhaps may be twenty times more out of control than you, rather than believe itself?

The mind's ineffectiveness is constantly endorsed by society. How often have people said to you, "Don't be silly. It is not logical. It is not allowed. It is not possible. It is not fair. It is not righteous. It is not this and it is not that." To compensate for your lack of ability to create reality through consciousness, the mind pretends that its desires are not important. Then if things do not materialize, the mind or ego can say, "I did not expect it anyway." We constantly adjust our expectation to accommodate disappointments.

My word is law unto me. By believing in the strength of my own reality, I materialize all that I want in life.

To experience your word as law you must begin to act and speak in a measured way. So often we tend to blurt out a promise or an idea and often we have little or no intention of following through. As you begin to see yourself as a powerhouse of consciousness you will actually begin to realize that you have power, power to change not only your life but the lives of others and

and the world around you.

As this power develops within you, the words you utter become symbols of that power. It is as if you are now a representative of the Force and what you say, you are able to deliver. It is a habit of the ego to make rash promises in order to gain acceptance to postpone or alleviate an awkward situation. Because the ego craves love and acceptance it will tend to try to accommodate everyone.

The function of the ego is to protect the identity's survival. In order to reduce the possibility of fatal conflict or danger to itself, it craves recognition and acceptance from as many people as possible. It does this in many covert ways. It shows the world a fake image of itself, in the hope that the world will accept it as good and loving and not threatening. For the ego knows that by coming from a position of expressed weakness, it will be more likely to be accepted by others, for they will feel more comfortable and less threatened. This helps the ego set up and endorse its own survival.

As you become more powerful you will begin to detach from the world, for it is basically weak. Part of this detachment is your ability to withdraw from the mind set and the feelings of the society around you. Remember, the way society controls you is that it implies that you are in some way responsible to it, or that at the very least you have a duty to it. This of course is not true and the God Force does not ask you to support, or not to support anything. Again, this is your decision. To accommodate this feeling, we tend to try to do what people want of us and have them like us. Once you go beyond worrying about whether people like you or not, then you can undercut their manipulation of you and establish a feeling of total independence. This is not a simple process, for remember, as a child you were programmed to seek approval by constantly doing what people wanted. Once you can go beyond that, the sky is the limit.

As you watch the manipulations of society you can understand them in a loving way. People have needs, they have fears, they go through their emotional struggles. Usually when a person's energy falls they begin to pull on you in some way. The trick is to support them without letting them pull you out of control.

This means dealing with them unemotionally, standing back somewhat and helping them raise their energy once more. The problem is that we are taught to use emotion to get what we want and so we tend to impose that on others, even if our request is not always reasonable. This is particularly true of family and friends. In those relationships we have a greater ability to manipulate and to be manipulated in return. I think it is possible to deal equitably with the loved ones around you without being pulled into a morass of obligation and duties that may not serve you.

Last year I asked a friend of mine to come to a seminar with me. He loved the idea and really wanted to come. It would have helped him. But he had to turn me down because the seminar fell on a holy day in his religion. Customarily, on that day his family would meet for some kind of worship and ceremonial meal. I asked him what was so special about that particular day. He replied that the day was considered holy because it was the day that God granted his tribe a great victory in battle. I was curious to know when the battle took place. My friend was not sure but it was at least two thousand years ago.

On investigation it turned out that my friend's tribe smashed the hell out of another tribe, killing thousands. And his tribe, being thankful at having massacred the opposition, decided that God granted them the victory and that henceforth that day of the year would be set aside for thanksgiving, ritual and ceremony. If I were God I would make a point of being out for that! But anyway, let us look at my friend's situation. Here was a grown man, extremely bright and creative, at the end of the twentieth century, unable to take an opportunity because he was worried about what his relatives would think of him if he did not show up for the ceremonial supper to celebrate a massacre. Why did he feel he had to celebrate it? Because the victory was good for the tribe so the victory became the will of God. Therefore, not celebrating the victory became contrary to the will of God. He was told so as a child by his mother and he swallowed it as real. As if the God Force in all its magnificence would give a damn about a tribal massacre and family supper!

The point is that if you enjoy following the family rituals then do them, but also allow yourself the latitude to give up on occasions when they do not suit your purpose. Try this: next Christmas, instead of going to your family home to eat some dumb turkey that has been shot full of toxins, tell them you are going to the Chinese take-out restaurant instead. Wait until about eight o'clock Christmas Eve before you inform them of your default. Then step back and watch the sparks fly!

Once you can unleash and detach from the craving of acceptance, you become free. You understand that what people think of you is a part of their evolution, but it is not a part of yours. Your identity and evolution are separate. As you become comfortable with this feeling, then you do not have to accommodate people. You do not have to be nice or charitable or kind or long-suffering or appeasing in any way. Remember, the God Force is impartial; it does not ask you to sacrifice yourself for others or to give up anything. If you choose to do so then that is your wish not the God Force's. The point is that we are brought up on the emotional manipulations of others. They use various forms of duty, honor, need, fear, tribal obligations, and negative emotion, to get us to do things they want us to do. Once you realize what they are doing to you, then you can detach and make decisions for yourself, even if those decisions are sometimes unpopular. And often they will be: people react passionately when you fail to respond to their manipulations.

As you become a powerful, independent, evolving being, you understand that you do not have to accommodate anyone, if that is not your wish. So, you do not have to promise people things to gain their acceptance, for you do not care if they accept you or not. The fact is, if you are expressing the God Force powerfully and if you develop within you a heightened sense of freedom, then people respond automatically. They perceive your strength and understand that you can stand alone. This relaxes them; it means they do not have to hold you up in any way. Remember, they will also have a natural tendency to try to appease and accommodate you. Your strength means they can relax and hopefully they can gain some energy from that.

Once you do not have to accommodate people, you can begin to act in a measured way. This means weighing event and decision in the light of your own needs, your own nurturing, your own growth. Then if you wish to help someone, you do so from your own volition, not from a feeling of having to or from their manipulation. By being forthright and acting in a measured way you move gently through the consciousness of the day. You do not run, you do not hurry and you set up time frames that are comfortable for you.

I am what I am and that is my evolution. What others perceive of me is a part of their evolution.

Once you settle into this detached power, then you begin to look at the words you utter. Do they come from strength, or are they designed to make others happy? Do you mean what you say, or are you just indulging yourself with half-truths and platitudes to avoid handling whatever is in front of you? As you look at that, you begin to see that often "talk" is just jibberish: promises that will never be kept, ideas that will never materialize, dreams that will never come true, and so on. Have you ever wondered why people talk like that? They do so because they do not experience their word as law. They do not expect their conscious thoughts to be manifest in reality, so they continue to play fantasy games which hark back to the non-reality of childhood and to the discomfort of not having the power to deliver, or acquire, in the physical plane the things they want. This weakens them.

As you move into the idea of your word as law, consider these things. Firstly, you will never, ever give your word to anyone in order to accommodate them. You will only do so if you endorse the promises you make. If people want you to do something against your wishes, you will explain, lovingly and politely, that you do not wish to be committed in that way. Next, you will give your word only rarely, and never when you do not have to. It is so simple to say to someone, "I am sorry but I cannot make that commitment at this time." Remember, the human mind is used to being put off. It constantly makes demands that it knows will not be fulfilled instantly. And it accepts 'later' as a natural part of reality. Choosing not to commit yourself reduces your chance of default. Next, if you ever give your word you will absolutely follow through on your commitment. If circumstances do not allow you to follow through, then you will use those circumstances to learn about the way consciousness flows and, next time, avoid a similiar situation.

Once you impose this kind of discipline in your dealings with others, you can begin to use it in relation to yourself. If you promise yourself that you will rise at dawn and run three miles, you do not allow the ego to entrap you with its excuses. And again you will not make promises to yourself unless you mean to keep them. As you become fierce in this kind of attitude then, gradually, your thoughts move from fantasy and chatter into an absolute manifestation of the God Force. Your word becomes law because you give meaning and importance to your word. It has reality. If you say it will be done, it will be done, no matter what.

Gradually you will experience giving your word to others, or to yourself, and witness the follow through. This experience becomes the affirmation. You will view yourself as a directed and powerful being. Each   you complete a commitment, you move further and further away from the debilitations of childhood. The center of your consciousness or intent will move from fantasy into reality.

Life is no longer a speculation or a dream; it is something that you actually experience. As your thoughtforms and words gain power, the parabola of energy on which they travel through Universal Law becomes shorter and denser. You can perceive your words and thoughts moving from consciousness into reality more quickly.

As you affirm, "I am power," the thoughtform moves from just mumblings into an absolute manifestation of your word as law. Pause for a moment and say those words to yourself aloud. Do you express them strongly or with a little hesitation? From this you can detect the measure of the strength of your word as law. The question is, can you deliver on an energy level? If not let us work on the way you use words and on your follow through. Soon you will experience a more resonant density to your consciousness that will materialize as benefits to you.

Affirmations of Individuality

I COMMUNICATE MY NEEDS. IN DOING SO I GET WHAT I WANT OUT OF LIFE.

I SPEAK AND ACT IN A MEASURED WAY. I CONTROL MY LIFE AT ALL TIMES. I MOVE THROUGH THIS DAY IN POWER AND STRENGTH AS AN INDIVIDUAL AND AT MY CONVENIENCE.

I AM WHAT I AM AND THAT IS MY EVOLUTION. WHAT OTHERS PERCEIVE OF ME IS A PART OF THEIR EVOLUTION.

I LOVE HUMANITY BY LETTING IT BE WHATEVER IT WANTS TO BE. I LOVE MYSELF BY BECOMING THAT WHICH I WISH TO BE.

7
AFFIRMATIONS OF THOUGHT
YOUR BATTLE PLAN

An affirmation of thought is basically an affirmation of consciousness. It is the lynch pin of your battle plan for self empowerment. Through it the *inner you* affirms a part of its self-image. The thoughts that go to create that self-image should be watched carefully, to make sure everything you express into consciousness empowers you.

Thought helps create, and is an integral part of your reality. Thought coupled with action creates your destiny.

Some years ago, I found myself at Kano airport in Northern Nigeria. My plane had been delayed for 48 hours with mechanical problems. When we were finally ready to take off again, we were led out onto the tarmac and told to wait. Then a very distinguished gent appeared from a hanger, riding a camel. He wore the most fantastic ceremonial regalia covered with gold braid. It seemed that he was very important, in local eyes anyway.

He trotted on to the tarmac carrying a long brass trumpet; it was easily ten feet in length. Pausing by our plane; he blew a ceremonial fart on his instrument and trotted off again. Baffled, I inquired as to what it all meant. It seems that in the 1950's a plane had crashed on take-off, and seven people were killed. The folk that administered the airport consulted with a local medicine man who declared that evil spirits had caused the crash. So it was decided to hire a trumpet player in order to scare off any negative influences prior to take off. He acted as a kind of rudimentary affirmation that all would be well in the future. Actually, it worked. There had been no more accidents at the airport since the fellow was engaged.

There was a downside though. The whole performance took about ten minutes. Meanwhile, all the passengers stood, luggage in hand, in a 120° heat on a runway as hot as a griddle. As we walked to the aircraft, I noticed that some of the people looked decidedly wobbly. I remember thinking that they must lose a few this way, especially the old folk.

As in affirmations of word, the key to your thoughts is what you believe and whether or not you feel that you have the ability to control your destiny. The unconscious man lives a life of chance: he does not understand how his destiny unfolds and presumes that the major events of his life are cast to luck. And thus he struggles. Gradually, through the bumps and bruises of daily life, the sleeping man gains a modicum of understanding, but it takes forever.

The conscious man, he who is alive to his development, understands that his life unfolds as an outer manifestation of inner thoughts, feelings and reality. And so this man lives his life in holy dedication to understanding himself. He sees his life as a symbol of the *inner self* and uses this symbol to strengthen and perfect what he is.

During the early years, the mind is fresh and clear of misfortune and all is positive and light. But as time goes on, the aches and pains of life create in the psyche deep rivers or tracks that cannot be easily rubbed out. For example, if, at the age of twelve, a young girl is frightened by someone on a street at night, it would be very hard for her to transcend that fear even though the same circumstances might never again happen in her lifetime. Even though she might be grown and able to care for herself, the negativity in the mind would be etched fiercely and dramatically, for it entered not only as a thought form but as a thought form accompanied by the extreme negative emotion of fear.

If she were to affirm "I am not scared of walking alone in the dark," she would have to recall the fact that she is scared, and this would only etch the pattern deeper. Thus, as we look at affirmations of thought, we must be sure to express those affirmations in a way that they will work for us.

As a teenager an individual has to reconcile all that he has learned and come into an identity of self. This process is usually very uncomfortable for it is hard to imagine not knowing who you are. During these years, and up to about the age of thirty, the individual's character and personality gradually unfold. In this crucial period the individual practices, through trial and error, creating a reality for himself. He sets a train of consciousness into motion and sees if it works the way he intends. Often there will be many changes in his life, many different people and many attempts to master life's processes. This is normal. Each time the individual faces adversity, he brings to that adversity his ability to transcend. His ability to be creative and to adapt is dominated by his experience of life so far, whatever that might be. And these confrontations, or trials in consciousness, more or less set down the quality of events the individual will experience for the rest of his life.

When he is about thirty-three years old his destiny is set in its general sense. It may change, but changing it takes great effort. It takes a complete realignment and usually that realignment is not taken by the individual voluntarily. Frequently it comes about through a major disaster in which the individual's life falls apart in some way. It could be accident or illness in which the individual faces death, or in some cases personal bankruptcy, divorce, or the misuse of alcohol or drugs.

Through facing the breakdown of the ego's self-image, the individual has the opportunity to realign and to create a new destiny for himself. Sometimes, this opportunity is missed and he will spin downwards for a while. If this downward parabola becomes constant, eventually the personal conflict is resolved by death. This is because the individual's *inner self*, having no place to go, and finding its spiritual progress stymied, gradually draws to itself a "way out." The transition from the physical plane allows the eternal self to regain control, and sometimes it seeks that option to extricate itself from an untenable situation.

As negativity gains a foothold within an individual, it becomes more and more powerful by virtue of the emotion created as a reaction to the ego's need to survive. Emotion is the very force that gives negativity its power. By being scared of something you make it real. Ironically, the individual's craving to survive creates his own destruction. For it is the ego's fear for its integrity that attracts its own destruction. In reality there is no death—but tell that to the ego!

The history of man is pervaded by stories of the great initiates dying and rising again. Talmmuz, Mithra, Adonis, the Nazarene, Hu the God of the Druids, all were said to have undergone the same process of transcending the ego. The ego had to release its grip on life and its terror of death in order for man to open himself to the power of good.

To shun negativity is only to give it credence. Once you can accept your fears as a part of what you are and look at them in a detached and loving way, they begin to dissipate. As they do so your projection into the Universal Law becomes stronger and more pleasing. Your life improves and the ego comes to realize that disaster is not necessarily a fact of life.

We can look at the world from a finite, egocentric view and see mayhem and disaster and say, "That is terrible," or we can look at it from an infinite view and see the beauty that there is in the learning process. Similarly, in your life, negativity assists you to become more Godlike but only if you do not struggle against it. The way to affirm your positive power is to laugh at your weakness and raise statues to your strengths.

Your ability to put consciousness into the Universal Law and have the Law respond is only exciting if it works! Anything else leads to frustration and a greater endorsement of the negativity. Each moment of your life is a programmed addition to the contents already laid down. You are affirming either a negative thought pattern or a positive one. There is nothing in between. Now when you see what destruction the power of the mind can create you should be pleased, for great manifestations of mayhem allow you to understand that there is also the potential for great positive results at the other end of the parabola.

The evil in the world allowed there to be saints, just as the failures of your life—and there really are none—allow you to create the groundwork for success. However, if you recall the disasters and say, "That is the energy pattern I experienced last time so I had better be careful this time, " you restrict your areas of personal development. Negative thought is self-fulfilling: the further you fall into negativity, the harder it is to climb out of the morass. The prophecy of negativity grows stronger and stronger and each event in your life serves to confirm its truth. To make affirmations of thought work, you have to create within you a parabola of hope and positive expectancy. The thoughtform has to become a natural habit that says, "There is a way and I will definitely find it." At first this thought is so weak it does not change your circumstances very much, but if you persevere and are patient with yourself, eventually the power of positive expectancy prevails. But think of this: if you create a thousand thoughts a day and you multiply that by the days of your life, you can see that the "feeling" base that you have created is substantial. It will only change given time. It takes tenacity of spirit to create triumphs. And yet if you look at the lives of the great men and women, the great achievers, you will see that each, without exception, faced and transcended tribulation, illness, bankruptcy or failure before they reached a pinnacle of human endeavor.

Before we go into the nature of thought, you might find it useful to take a piece of paper and write down your greatest disasters. Title them as if they were great motion pictures. Give the disaster a catchy name like, "The day I actually ate the neighbor's canary." Create three columns. Put the title in the first column, put the consequences or results of your actions—what actually happened—in the second column. For example, "I was sued by my neighbor," and "I had indigestion for a week." Then in the third column write down what you learned from the experience. For each of the disasters was a lesson. You signed up for a course in daily life. The only bad thing that could possibly happen is that you went on the course, paid to attend but did not get the message. Failure to "get it" brings the lessons round again and again in various forms. This is because they lie in the *inner you* as conflicts or weakness and eventually they rise like miasma from a swamp and pull to you events that reflect their characteristics.

Sometimes the Universal Law has a way of taking you extremely literally and it creates events for you that are exact reflections of what you are thinking, but not necessarily what you had in mind.

I was lecturing at a church on the East Coast of the United States and while I waited in a back room for the lecture to start, the phone rang. A woman with a resounding voice informed me that she was a spiritual teacher in those parts and she gave me to understand that she was making a special journey across town to grant me an audience.

Normally I like to meet other lecturers. I enjoy finding out where they are at and how they think. But on this occasion I would have been perfectly happy to give the proposed meeting a miss.

By the time the lecture started, she had not as yet shown up, and I lived in the hope that she had changed her mind. I had been lecturing for about forty minutes when there was a tremendous clatter at the back of the church and the woman walked in. She was enormous, at least three hundred pounds, maybe four. Vast acres of flesh hung round her body incoherently.

In her mind she had decided to create an impression. Instead of slipping quietly into the back row, she began a slow and somber progress down the main aisle. I did not have any comment or judgment to make about her size, but if you have ever done any public speaking you will know how distracting it is if someone walks in late. You tend to lose your train of thought.

Every step she took resounded throughout the church, echoing in the rafters. The audience all turned round to see who it was, and by now my lecture had more or less spluttered to a halt. The whole performance of her entrance was designed to gain attention, and that it did. As she walked, she alternately lunged her huge legs cautiously forward, simultaneously rotating the appropriate hip. Meanwhile the rest of her body did its very best to follow.

Everything proceeded fairly well until she got to within five rows of the front. By now she was a bit embarrassed that she had brought the whole lecture to a standstill, so she quickened her pace. Fatal. One of the parishoners had left a large wicker hand-basket in the aisle. The woman never saw it. She gave one hell of a "clunk" with her foot then, lurching forward, she vainly rotated her arms in an elusive search for stability.

As you know, when disaster strikes things tend to go in slow-motion. I stood at the podium, suspended in time, watching helplessly as the woman titter-tottered over a non-existent center of gravity and finally fell flat on her back. She lay there like Moby Dick.

Hastily, six of the more sturdy members of the congregation rushed to her aid: The problem was that the flesh of her body had finally found its true resting place, close to ground-zero, and it steadfastly refused to be lifted back to the normal vertical position.

Well, to cut a long story short we finally got her on her feet and into one of the pews and the lecture continued. But the embarrassment of the poor woman was so intense that everyone felt extremely uncomfortable. I cracked up so badly, I had to call a ten minute break. Interestingly enough, the woman used that as an excuse to beat a retreat and I never did get to meet her properly.

Her affirmation that she wanted to create an impression must not have been clear to the Universal Law, so it did the best it could to accommodate her. I am sure she will never forget that day and the event would probably haunt her forevermore, resting near the top of her greatest disasters list. Yet I am sure that if she had a sense of humor she would shrug it off as an exercise in daily life.

By looking at the lessons of life in this way you see them in a clear light. If, say, you were a great troublemaker, you could see the weakness of that pattern and learn from it. Plus you have pleasure in realizing that the people in the film of your greatest disasters, its characters, were actually in a film of their own. And if we all create our own reality then they also created theirs, pulling you into their life. They put into the Universal Law, "Give me turmoil," and you very kindly showed up at the right time, creating for them the kind of disaster they were looking for. You acted as a cosmic "rent a problem" and they learned about themselves. Everything in consciousness is relative, meaning that they had as much responsibility for the event as you did. Even if on the surface they look like innocent victims, there are none.

I grant myself forgiveness and complete absolution. For my energy has now risen above and beyond any errors I may have made in the past.

If you will take a few moments to clear out some of the old debris and love yourself for your weaknesses, you will learn to exhibit the same benign magnanimity that the God Force has for you. The fact that you are not perfect is just dandy, for if you were perfect, you would not be on the earth plane. You would not bother to be here.

The lessons of the earth plane are important. Have you ever wondered why the God Force allows such mayhem to exist? Either the God Force sees it as helpful and beautiful, or it does not. If it does not see it as useful, why does the God Force not fix it? The answer of course is that it cannot. Once the evolution of man was put into progress the God Force had to back out and let us all get on with it. I am convinced that the intrinsic weakness of the ego is forseen. Yet the species has to survive and so whatever difficulties we have to transcend are just a natural part of the course.

Once you can take this benign overview of the world and your life, the negativity laid down over the years begins to lessen and you detach yourself from the destiny of man. This, in turn, helps you to transcend, and once you have made this step an affirmation of thought has a chance.

Thought is empowered mainly in three ways. First, it is empowered by the quality of the Life Force you maintain. It is as though the thought forms you create have an intrinsic value or integrity, and that integrity is in part sustained by the Life Force within the thought. The thought form is created through consciousness, but is energized by Life Force. You can create an affirmation of great beauty, but if it has little Life Force it will not come to pass. You can affirm, "This is my day and I feel good," and if there is no light in the thought it will dissipate quickly and your mood will change. It is the Life Force in the thought that makes it dynamic.

Consider the thought to be like an arrow. As a thought leaves the bow of your mind, its intrinsic strength dissipates according to the amount of life force it contains. That Life Force is created by you. If your energy is low, the quantum of power you create in the thought is also low. There is nothing more powerful than your inner Life Force. It is the very essence of your being and it is that part of you that will take you outside and beyond the mundane, day-to-day living. It is that part that connects you to all things, the voice that calls to you from infinity and is only sometimes heard.

The Life Force in your thoughts is a measure of your personal power. You cannot be effective in the dimension of the physical plane without power. If power bothers you, if you feel power is not holy or is against the will of God or that somehow you will not be saved if you become powerful, then you do not understand the Universal Law. Just because power is misused in the world does not mean it will corrupt you. It is quite possible, given understanding and love, to become powerful and not to misuse it. But if you will not concentrate and work on your power then you are like the sleeping man, unable through belief patterns or commitment to control his life.

The *power* of your Life Force is expressed in several ways. It is expressed first through your body. Whatever you are, whatever you create in this life will have the fingerprint or mark of your body's energy on it. There is no avoiding it. You cannot reach a peak within yourself if you have not worked on your body and taken it to its highest level. The main lessons of the physical plane are naturally learned through the body. If you do not deal with your body—if you find it boring, if it scares you, or if you feel you are so much a part of higher things that handling the physical body is not important—then you have missed the lesson of this plane. Imagine looking back over your life and over all the effort it entailed saying, "If only I had not been so silly. If only I had not been so phony in my spirituality, if only I had not avoided the physical. If only..."

To be fully in the physical world you have to become accomplished in the ways of the earth plane. This includes understanding the world, developing intellect and creativity, going beyond emotion, being in control of your finances and being in control of your physical body. Control means that you work on your body constantly. It does not mean there will be no imbalances; it just means that you take responsibility for those imbalances. You have to work on them and you do so in a disciplined way, taking the consequences when you do not. The Life Force of the body gives resonance to your thought form, gives it intrinsic power. It allows thought to mingle with the Universal Law and to pull to you the opportunities you seek.

Secondly, your Life Force is affected and expressed through emotion. As you express emotion the feeling around you changes and grows turbulent. Consequently the reality you draw towards you enters that turbulence and is rearranged or deflected by the resulting imbalance in yourself. Within moments your body begins to react adversely, and your thought form projections become brittle. Your ability to control the events around you is lost, for the power of your consciousness is vastly diminished.

If you are exposed to negative emotion for long enough, you lose your ability to control and you fall prey to chance. Your chance experience will be congruent with the "out-of-control" energy you express.

By calming your emotions and seeing life as beautiful, you create an incubator in which your affirmations of thought will grow. The dimension of feelings around you begins to calm and regains its natural resonance. As you become calmer, the ego backs off and you can see things as they really are, rather than through the energy of the ego which holds countless opinions about your life, much of them inaccurate.

> *I am open to this day.*
> *My life is in flow.*
> *I resonate in the beauty of my inner calm.*

The emotions you express are just responses to the ego's uncertainty about life. Because the ego is constantly watching for the safest path, it tries desperately to see round corners. The ego plays a game called, "what if." From past experiences it constructs probability patterns which result in more worry and negative emotion.

Take a moment to truly accept your own death. Feel its transcendent quality. See how change is a part of the natural order and know from deep within yourself that you do not actually die. You will never be more alive than the moment after your body closes down. At that point you will move on to whatever evolution you have set for yourself through power in this world. That is the only important factor, the one that you will work on constantly from this day to your last.

Si uoy nihtiw ecroF efiL eht srewopme taht rotcaf driht ehT taht tnatropmi yrev si tI .yhposolihp evitanretla eht llac I tahw -solihp a ton ,uoy rof skrow taht efil fo yhposolihp a etaerc uoy elcriC eht fo sfeileb eht morf nwod-em-dnah a tsuj si taht yhpo eht wolla uoy yaw lanigiro na ni efil ruoy gnivil yB .elpoeP syaw ni dna ylsuoenatnops uoy ot dnopser ot waL lasrevinU .ecneirepxe ton od srehto

In developing a philosophy of life I feel it is best to discard the restrictive parts of some of the man-made religions. This does not necessarily mean you have to throw out all that is written in the holy books, but it means that you just take from them the bits that serve you, those parts that are self-empowering, and you dump anything that does not have your interest at heart.

By creating a philosophy that is truly your own, you gain the freedom to think about your life and to develop it in the direction that pleases you.

The trick is to develop a kind of spiritual solitude, living your own life, living your own beliefs and just not telling others what it is you do. Once you develop that kind of originality and belief in yourself, what others think and do will not bother you. You will be happy if they go their own way. Moreover, you will prove your love by leaving them alone, will you not?

To the Universal Law, *what* you believe does not matter—just that it works for you. In the old days, religions tried to capture truth by controlling the common man's access to "knowledge." The churches monopolized truth to suit their ends. They told the people that there was a truth that God liked (whatever teaching the church dreamed up) and there was a truth that God did not like (any teaching that contradicted the church.) But in reality there is no absolute truth, only millions and millions of various opinions, each being true to the individual. And the God Force is not emotionally involved in what you believe.

In the spirit dimensions beyond earth whatever you believe is reflected back to you and the ambience or conditions of the place in which a spirit exists is created solely as a result of the collective feelings of the spirits gathered there. If a dimension is restrictive it will look gray and drab but the spirits there will not see its ugliness. Their dimension is truth to them. Beyond the drab areas are celestial heavens in which all is beauty and light. It is so because the spirits there endorse freedom and they hold to a philosophy that liberates rather than restricts. Because their feelings are expansive and accepting of each other, the light reflects this in the beauty of their surroundings. There are few rules and regulations, save that each spirit endorses goodness expressed as unconditional love.

The celestial spirits have evolved a long way from the beliefs of man and so their ability to express unconditional love is immense. When I first glimpsed one of these dimensions I realized how vital it was for humans to move away from stereotypes we think are the truth towards a philosophy that first endorses ourselves and eventually, as we become comfortable with that, endorses everyone else. The more you can move from the Circle mind-set into your own philosophy the more celestial you become. In doing so you have to have the courage of your own convictions.

If, for example, you rise at 3 a.m. in the morning and eat a piece of French bread filled with a bar of chocolate, alfalfa sprouts, a line of mustard and a dollop of ketchup, then that is your philosophy. Others may think you are crazy, but to you the meal helps you to feel powerful in your day. So do it!

By developing your own philosophy you free yourself from convention and a thousand years of puerile tradition. Is it not true that when you meet a person who is a little crazy you generally find they are a lot of fun? They seem to take life in stride. Their looniness sustains them. That is philosophy.

My philosophy is truth unto me. Through expressing my individuality I become free.

Societies, governments, and the associations of man call upon you to endorse them and abandon your own dream to work for theirs. If you fall for this your Life Force will be reduced and your power through the earth plane is disenfranchised. You are not living and attending to your own will; you are living the will of others.

Let us look at some of the common misconceptions about society and, especially, governments. Then let us consider how to develop a philosophy that is free yet does not infringe on others.

First, if you think the government acts in your interest, forget it. All governments are a part of "tick-tock" and act for themselves, even if they pretend otherwise. The level of manipulation they impose on their people is enough to dominate them without causing mass disobedience. And what gives a government power is money—the money it gets from you. It has no divine right to that money, nor do you have any spiritual duty to pay. But once the government has your money it uses it to create institutions (the police, the IRS, the CIA, the military) that force you into giving it even more money.

The government of the United States, for example, is dominated by white, Caucasian males who lean politically to the right (even if they are Democrats) and parrot the will of the "families." The laws and the courts reflect the views of these men. If you are neither white, nor male, if you are an individual, if you happen to be in a minority, or a left-winger, the government passes few laws that have your interest at heart. And it performs almost no function that people could not perform for themselves.

The government creates rules and regulations to suit itself. There are over a million in the U.S. statute books. The rules come out of its own vested interest. You have probably noticed that no matter what party is in power things do not change very much. This is because all of the major political parties are influenced by the Circle mind set and the laws they pass reflect that influence. If you do not conform, the government uses threats to subjugate you. It makes you pay for all sorts of things that you do not need or want. Further, the government allows the states to create regulations, laws and taxes and it allows those bodies the power to control you also.

In the town I live in you cannot buy a bottle of beer in a store on Sunday. This law reflects the fundamentalist opinion that beer on Sunday is bad and needs to be controlled. The town has just under 4,000 residents of which less than 50 per cent are practicing fundamentalists and even fewer are fundamentalists. On any given Sunday the town has an additional 5000 visitors, some of whom are probably fundamentalists but most of whom come here for skiing and to have fun. So the will of a few hundred people is imposed on perhaps as many as a half million a year. There is absolutely nothing that the majority can do about it.

This kind of infringement is repeated by governments over and over again. To believe that the government is good and that it has your interest at heart is naive. History shows us that all governments will let you down all of the time. For example, in the United States in the 1930's President Franklin D. Roosevelt, who was considered an honest leader, presided over a three billion dollar robbery of the American people. The Great Depression gripped the country and Roosevelt asked the government to pass a law forcing Americans to return all their gold to the government at the bargain price of $20.67 an ounce. As soon as Roosevelt had all the gold he raised the price to $35 per ounce and turned a handsome three billion dollar profit.

If you lived during that time and had your own philosophy, you would not have fallen for that. You would have shipped your gold out of the country before the bill was passed and placed it on deposit somewhere else as did many others. Because of your philosophy you would have been a lot richer, and more free, than those who were robbed.

Society promotes the idea that there is a kind of spiritual duty to obey it. And yet, when you look at what you are asked to condone, you can see that much of it is unjust—a blatant rip-off. Now, should you protest or organize or defy the law? Hell no! You make a mistake if you do. The government relies on people not knowing what is going on and ensures that those who do will not have the courage to protest. If you do protest, the government will come down on you like a ton of bricks. It has to. By punishing the individual it terrorizes the majority into conforming.

The name of the game is to take the Taoist view and maintain as low a profile as possible. For example, if you do not vote you are not called for jury duty. I have never voted for anything, ever. That is my philosophy. I feel that voting just encourages them. Is this against the law? No. If you do not want to vote you do not have to. By the way, another way to avoid jury duty is to tell them you are Taoist. Taoists do not believe in sin. So you tell the court that you would love to serve as a jurist but that as a Taoist you will have to find the defendant "not guilty" because that is your philosophy. The prosecuting attorney, who needs to get a conviction to keep his job, will release you from jury duty in no time.

There is always a way. During the Vietnam war I was friends with an American who lived in London. The draft board found him eventually and he was called for an interview at the Embassy in Grosvenor Square. Clearly, my friend was not into getting shot and he did not support the government's actions against the people of Vietnam. The day before the interview he had his hair dyed light purple. Then he spent an hour at a theatrical costumers renting a velvet cape and a pair of crushed velveteen knickerbockers. He rounded off his outfit with a charming pair of satin slippers with silver buckles. On the morning of the interview he got a facial at the local beauty shop and had himself made up. Then he found a nice pink bow and tied it to the collar of his little dog.

My friend, who was a macho two-hundred-fifty pounds, minced into the interview saying how much he would love to join "the boys" in Southeast Asia. He was promptly declared invalid on account of the fact that the U.S. army does not recruit homosexuals. Was he breaking the law? No. It was not his fault that the recruiting officer thought he was gay. In fact, when the recruiting officer asked him if he were gay, my friend replied, "What do you think?" Now that is philosophy.

The point is that we always think of the government as a superpower that can trample us into the dust and we meekly acquiesce to its demands. Once you have philosophy you will understand that there is basically no government, just a group of bureaucrats most of whom are "tick-tocking" through to their pensions by causing as few waves as possible—that is your trumpcard. The government has to bend over backwards to appear fair, spending millions of dollars of your money on public relations. It knows that it is manipulating the people, but the government figures that as long as it *pretends* to be fair no one will notice that it is in fact robbing them blind.

You have to obey the government's laws because being outside the law will cause you an imbalance that will eventually draw attention from one of the law-enforcement agencies who delight in antagonizing you. A Taoist precept states that by placing yourself underneath you are in effect on top. By seeming to be little and insignificant you set yourself free. The tallest tree is chopped down; the gnarled stump is left alone.

But, you may say, how do we ever change things for the better? The fact is that things overall do not change for the better, only individuals do. Nothing stops you from changing your whole life into an incredible symphony of success. But appealing to the government will get you nowhere. If you try to change a law, a hundred people will jump up and try to change it back again. The energy you dissipate is not worth the effort. That is why the Taoist sages wound up living in the forest: conscious man has to be detached and on his own in order to reach a higher level of energy.

I truly accept the world the way it is. By becoming detached I reach a higher level of energy within me.

Move silently through life. Keep the major part of your thoughts and actions to yourself. Never tell people what you know. By keeping silent you avoid the tentacles people place on you. You develop intrinsic "mystery." Once you become mysterious you gain power. First, you do not dissipate yourself in idle chatter and, secondly, people grant you a power that is often greater than that which you actually maintain. Consider the legendary warriors of old whose prowess in battle preceded them. They rarely had to fight. People respected their reputation and, because the warriors had philosophy no one dared to challenge them.

Developing mystery is especially important for women. The things not known about a woman make her alluring and exciting to be with. A woman should have her methods of self-healing, nurturing, expressing power, but these should be her secret. It should be her world and the man in her life, if there is one, should never be allowed access to those secrets. If a woman becomes too accessible she loses that magic or mystery and finds her ability to get what she wants greatly diminished.

Finally, before we close this section on developing an alternative philosophy, let me make two points. First, I think it is vital that your philosophy not infringe on others. It should express the originality and experience you have developed over the years, but you have to be careful not to create waves. Obey the laws when you have to. Remember that only a fool stands and fights; the sage walks away. Confrontation is a trap and should be avoided at all costs. When you do not feel the need to change things, you become free. You stop "being in the result" and instead concentrate on "being." Thus you move away from the pressure of struggle and into flow, which is your ultimate goal.

Second, you have to consider yourself spiritually. If you see yourself as a part of the God Force, then its power is with you. If you see yourself as separate from the God Force or as unworthy in some way, then your thoughts have less strength. (We will deal with this topic more fully in the next chapter under the heading "identity.") It is important to see your life as an infinite expression of the beauty that is in all things. To do this you have to detach from all the emotion-driven movements about world peace, poverty and nuclear bombs. These movements derive from a spiritual weakness. They reflect the discomfort people feel and are a waste of time until the hierarchies that control the situation decide to get involved. That is why these movements have little or no impact. If you want world peace, as I do, become powerful. Feel the limitlessness inside yourself and barge into the war-maker's office, grab him by the scruff of the neck and say, "Stop it, or else!"

The alternative is to respect the physical plane and see it as the infinite lesson that it actually is. Understand that peace will come in time but first we have to evolve through our discomforts. Let me explain. In the world today there are millions of souls completing their evolution. They are here to be in the metaphysical "wrap and pack show." Alongside these souls are billions of others which are just beginning their evolution in the physical plane and will evolve in the millenia to come through reincarnations. These souls are here to observe the potential that they can actually achieve. That is all. They are not expected to reach great heights. Their evolution deals with understanding the basic things in life: tribal ways, physical body, sexuality, poverty and strife of various kinds.

The Second World War cleared the way for man's evolution to rapidly progress. As evolved souls began to feel their freedom, their creativity knew no bounds. They set themselves on the path to total freedom and enlightenment—beyond the usual restrictions that are the lessons of the physical. They invented television and in one generation their invention was granted to everyone. It allowed the others an understanding of what could be. It also showed the world that we are all one, linked by the same Universal Energy. And it showed us that our evolutions are separate.

Tribal man, watching a flickering black-and-white TV, went through a rapid change of consciousness. He became aware of a vision beyond his mundane circumstance, and he in turn aspired to higher things. But he did not have the energy to pull it off, which caused him negative yearning. There is so much strife in the world because these souls are struggling to achieve a dimension of consciousness that is beyond them. They have been sold the glamor and the "razamataz" but no one showed them how to get it.

As the evolved souls became more and more enlightened they began to change the destiny of the world on an inner level. Since the mid-1970's the evolution of the world has accelerated faster and faster. You will have noticed it. Things are becoming harder and harder to maintain. The energy differential between evolved souls and tribal man is widening. As it does so the strife of the world increases because man's discomfort is accentuated by the differential. The destiny of man is like a wind blowing faster and faster. Only the very strong will maintain, the rest will have to recede. As they do so there will be more war, increased poverty, and greater political fragmentation.

Have you ever wondered why America and the West are disliked by the Third World countries and other small nations? It is because they see the lifestyle and the abundance that comes from creativity and effort and fear that they will never achieve this for themselves. As the Western people evolved, they shared their abundance with the rest of the world in the greatest transfer of wealth in the history of man. Much of the money was just given and much was lent on "easy terms." Those souls that were in a higher evolution than the rest, and America along with other major trading nations, tried to buy the same evolution for poorer nations, partly out of a sense of guilt and partly because it was politically advantageous to enslave the world in debt. Albania is almost the only country that did not accept the Western societies' handout and the only reason it did not get any money was because no one could find the place. Those that did receive the money spent it on a frivolous orgy of self-aggrandizement. The money still had to be paid back. The citizens of those Third World countries are now forced to foot the bill for the juvenile ego trips of their leaders. Those citizens resent America and the West for the misused gifts, often claiming that they would rather accept the extreme manipulation of Communism than to have to face the fact that their leaders let them down.

Everyone wants world peace and the abolition of poverty, but the energy of the world will not allow it as yet. We have to be patient. It is futile to hanker for a concept that is not a part of the evolution of the people at this time. It would be like insisting that terrorists become vegetarians who meditate. Forget it!

If you get sucked into the emotion of these social movements it will hinder your evolution. The mind has a tendency to put off personal action and go for the concept because that involves no personal risk or effort. By embracing such causes you will see the world in a negative light and gradually your attitude in your own life will reflect the same weakness. This may carry you down on a spiral of hopelessness. I would not want that for you.

Let us imagine that the God Force decided one morning to declare world peace and then somehow manipulated everyone into being peaceful. Would your life really change that much? It is peaceful now, is it not? You would find yourself in your home, with your loved ones, eating breakfast perhaps, discussing life, watching TV or whatever. It would be no different. So why get all wrapped up emotionally about something you already have?

To become powerful you have to concentrate on yourself and allow the world its evolution. By concentrating on yourself you become strong; then you can truly help the people. Metaphysically, there is really no other way. And you have only a short time to pull it off. Any negative yearning or wasted effort and you are "dead in the water." Your evolution is to create that crescendo of energy in yourself and to evolve out of the physical to become a part of the Higher Power. That is your final destiny! Accept it lovingly, accept it as your affirmation of thought, and understand that everything in the world is as it should be. In this way you claim your true infinity.

---

1 move silently through life. This allows me to change into what 1 am becoming. — Through silence 1 develop an alternative philosophy.

8
EMPOWERMENT THROUGH UNDERSTANDING VARIANCE AND CONCENTRATION

The next aspect that affects the thought form power within you is called *variance*. Variance is the difference between what you actually are and what the ego or personality thinks you are. We each hold opinions about ourselves, but the Higher Self or *inner you* lives in the now. It is real and it lives in truth. If what you believe about yourself is greatly different from what is actually true, a subtle tension arises within you that does not allow your consciousness to have all the power it should.

The tension between your ego's desires and your ability to manifest those desires creates a variance or deficiency within you. That deficiency is accentuated by the difference between the quality of life you actually live (what is real) and your thought forms which may include a large element of fantasy.

By living in fantasy what you express is weakened because the *inner you* knows that you just do not believe it and that it is not true. So rather than concentrating on what empowers, you dissipate energy on chatter and on fantasies which you have no intention of materializing.

Sometimes you create variance by expanding your lifestyle beyond what you can handle. This will also cause imbalance for you will find yourself stumbling to catch up. You will try to materialize the mental image you have of yourself and your thought forms will lose intensity. This type of variance is very common in the area of finances. We create an image of the lifestyle we want and often we commit to our expenditure, without really having the wherewithal to pay for our desires.

Then we cast our fate with the generosity of the Universal Law and hope for the best, not realizing that being out of control actually destroys our ability to make money and to pull opportunities to us. The result is that we find ourselves scrambling even more.

The very fact that you are desperate to close a deal so that you can pay the rent pushes it away. Metaphysically it hops up the road in front of you. The reason is that in order for people to give you their money they have to feel secure. When you are out of control they pick up on your emotions and back away. The same happens in negotiating—when you want something, the other people in the deal know it, and it either costs you more or something happens to destroy the deal. The way to negotiate is to release any emotion about the deal and be prepared to walk away. Then you are in control and the power is with you.

Imagine yourself by a fountain. That fountain is your Higher Self, your source of power. If you live in the now and accept yourself in truth, you stand in the center of the fountain and have maximum power. If you live in the fantasy of your ego's image of you, you drift away from the fountain and so your consciousness becomes oblique and loses force. It is as though you were asking the Universal Law to endorse a lie or a fake image of yourself. Remember, the Universal Law will give you whatever you believe in. But when living in the puffery of the ego, we play a game that creates a deficiency or weakness in the energy of our thought forms.

It is strengthening to develop a consciousness that more closely resembles who you really are. This does not mean you should not visualize or create in your mind's eye those things that you want to become. But often individuals live only in their fantasies. It is not that fantasy cannot be ultimately realized; the problem is that usually the individual does not really believe his fantasy. Not believing it ensures that it will never happen. In addition, by being so far removed from reality in day-to-day life, it is hard for him to become strong.

The Life Force that is around you—in nature, in your home,

in your relationships, in your sexuality, in your creativity—assists you as an individual. If your life is at a variance with your fantasy, not only do you dissipate the power of your visions, but you also fail to gain energy from your surroundings because you are basically not living in them. Your mind is someplace else.

It is hard for people to live in the real world for in doing so they have to get into eye-to-eye contact with the facts. One must ask, "Where am I right now? What do I have so far? What am I, really?" Now, if you have courage to face yourself and to be content with all that you have not-as-yet-achieved, then you grasp the power of the moment—beyond the games of the ego and the social pressures that require you to pretend to be something you are not.

I accept who I am and the reality in which I live. Through patience I achieve all that I desire.

Stardom consciousness, the feeling that someday someone will discover you, is another good example of variance. The ego adjusts to failure by living in fantasy. It is as if the ego knows that it cannot be bothered to succeed and, because it does not like to face that fact, it tells itself a lie. The ego says, "One day I will be discovered and I will become successful and be a great star"—therefore the ego does not have to take any real action. Being discovered does not entail working or putting in concentrated effort. Many people bring the same attitude to spirituality. They believe that enlightenment should be graciously bestowed upon them, with minimal participation on their part. That is why gurus are so popular. The student can sit at the foot of the guru and have the sage's godliness transferred to him with no effort. Instant enlightenment, just add water!

As you work with affirmations you will have to look at what is fantasy and what is fact. As a child of the Universe you should never be afraid to admit where you are, for there is a very special energy in that. In cosmic evolution we put ourselves into energy patterns that are slightly ahead of us. In this way we have something to grow into. The difficulty is that we judge ourselves in light of the energy that surrounds us and it makes us feel inadequate. In such circumstances it is hard to see ourselves as beautiful. Yet what you are is what you are. By accepting that you can go on to better things, you will gain the strength to affirm that you are becoming more — becoming a part of another dimension, a higher plane of living. However, if the dimension you think you are heading towards is very far from where you are now, your mind will intellectualize your being there, but the *inner you* will not believe it possible. Hence, with your thought affirmations you should create thought forms slightly beyond, but close to, where you are now.

Imagine that for the last ten years you have been driving a broken down rust-bucket of a car. You have done so because you didn't have much money, or when you had money you didn't consider it important to buy a new car. Those ten years have set up a pattern inside you. The countless times you had to push the car to start it or tinkered with the carburetor in the freezing snow, the way the wind whistles through the floorboards, the symphonic rattles, the jarring bumps and bangs as it splutters along the highways and byways — these are a part of your life. To affirm, "I will be driving a Cadillac," is so far from your current experience it is almost impossible to materialize. The rut in your consciousness after ten years of "rattle and roll" cannot be transcended by a single thought that has little intensity. And if the thoughtform is actually, "I am driving a Cadillac," your fantasy does not allow space for transformation, and you will be in your rust-bucket for another ten years.

Affirmations of thought must be strong in order to push through the resistance created by past programming. The affirmation must be close to reality. It would make sense to affirm, "Within thirty days I will release this old rust-bucket and I will pull to me — or manifest — a modern, clean, reliable car."

This affirmation has possibilities. For it asks, not for a great quantum leap, but for a gradual change.

The history of man and the development of spirituality and consciousness show that growth has been progressive. As man has become more aware of himself, building on past achievements, the pace has begun to quicken. Still, each gain lies close to the previous boundary. In your life you should look for gradual change and take the time to acknowledge that progress, step by step. Be sure that when you create affirmations of thought, what you affirm is close to what you actually have so that the Universal Law can materialize your wishes.

The Life Force or strength of your thought forms is ultimately linked to *identity*, or the strength of the connection you have to life and the God Force. If you see the God Force or Life Force as outside of yourself, your thought forms express themselves obliquely. That obliqueness will hold you in place and keep you involved in your present circumstances.

It is as if the thought form must, by its very nature, cross in front of you and in the crossing stop your forward progress. The identity factor becomes stronger as you grow older and are ready to reconcile yourself to success. The issue is not so much a factor before age thirty-three or for those whose lives follow a different evolution.

The obliqueness created by a lack of identity with the God Force is fine in the early years, because it keeps you from going ahead too quickly and forces you to deal with day-to-day life. However, as the sleeping man wakes and realizes that the God Force is not outside of himself, is not an authority over him—that in fact the God Force is an inner power—then his thought forms change dramatically. It is as if the sleeping man were to suddenly give himself permission to be free—to exist as a part of all things, as an individual, not as a part of someone else's program. The history of man reveals that the beginnings of knowledge and metaphysics coincide around 500 BC. At this time about a half dozen masters, including Buddha, Zoroaster, and Lao Tzu, all appeared at once. This quickened the evolution of man and allowed the concept of the sanctity of man to develop. But slavery did not disappear until man developed self-image and the realization that he is a part of the God Force and not just chattel at someone's disposal.

The difficulty then, in general, is that once the sleeping man wakes to the reality of his *inner force*, he has to release whatever he believed in the past. Old beliefs feel safe and comfortable. The new thoughts will be unexplored and awkward at first and the sleeping man will tend to drift away from the people to whom he is accustomed, thus feeling fear and loneliness.

The identity factor allows for the Life Force in your thoughts to be expressed with an integrity that does not overly confine or control it. Once your thought identifies with the *inner force*, it gains power. It may do as it wishes. You are therefore affirming, "I am God." That can be hard, for as children we are often taught that we are close to worthless and that God is a big daddy seated someplace lording over us. Not so.

By identifying with the God Force you acknowledge your spiritual heritage. You allow yourself to be, without having to ask permission. You are what you are and, as a part of all things, you have intrinsic rights. Once identity is established, once you know absolutely that you are the God Force within, then gradually you can give yourself permission to succeed and to become whatever it is you want to become, away from the desires, thoughts and manipulations of others. What you are to become is private to you and only really you know what path your life, destiny and spiritual growth will take. You stand alone, apart from others, beyond what others think of you, beyond what they want of you, beyond what they say you should do, and very far beyond other's dogmas and spiritual manipulations. You have integrity. You are not necessarily whole or perfect, and yet there is a part of you that is very beautiful. That part creates the bridge that takes you from one enlightening experience to the next, to places in the heart so far from day-to-day concerns that the beliefs of the sleeping man mean nothing to you and they have no adverse emotional effect. This process of identifying can take many years or it can be accomplished quickly, for each person is different. But it takes courage, for once it is complete you stand alone.

The way to enhance your identity with the God Force is to begin to release ego and melt into the infinity of all things. This means practicing being alone with yourself. There is a great power in solitude, for it allows you to acknowledge God. Take time to be with nature and as you walk, watch how, for example, a small bird expresses identity. It does so freely because it does not have an opinion about itself. It has none of the Self-consciousness that we humans have. In not having opinions it acts naturally. You too can achieve the same exhilaration of life.

To develop identity you must give yourself permission to create absolute freedom in your life, and to cultivate a way of life that separates you from the evolution of others. You cannot change the nature of the Circle and the philosophy of its people; all you can do is withdraw within your own power. Remember: no one is testing you. The God Force does not test us, nor ask us to give up or struggle or sacrifice. Only man creates struggle for himself and instead of taking responsibility for his problems he blames the God Force, or chance.

The Life Force is also enhanced by your *congruence* with it. Identifying is saying, "I know it is there within me." Congruence is living and breathing the God Force within. That means developing a lifestyle or philosophy that includes honoring the Life Force within you, and that exemplifies courage. You will have to put your life on the line, metaphysically trusting 100 per cent in the God Force to provide your needs and to keep you safe. But in adopting this way of life, you create a power massive and magnanimous enough to sustain you. Moreover, your perception and ability to understand what is going on around you will increase dramatically.

With your originality and individual philosophy of life, you create a congruence with the infinity in all things regardless of the circumstances around you. The God Force is spontaneous, original and outside the confines of opinions and the mind. By living your life without judgment—detached, living moment-to-moment—you create a similiar spontaneity and your congruence with this force gradually becomes stronger.

Try this simple exercise. Sit in front of a full-length mirror, put on some relaxing music, close your eyes and go into meditation. Once relaxed, open your eyes again and wait a moment. Then stare at yourself in the mirror without moving and, if possible, without blinking.

In the mirror you   notice your features change as your personality relaxes through the meditation. You will have the eerie feeling of not knowing who you are looking at. As you lose yourself the infinity within you will become apparent. Many experience a sense of timelessness or even ecstasy.

Once you realize that you are a timeless immortal within a body, try the following exercise. For the next thirty days totally change the pattern of your life. Get up at a different time. Go to bed later or earlier. Do not do any of the things you normally do. Talk to none of your friends. Avoid newspapers, radio and television. Dress differently and change your eating habits. Spend time on your own in silent meditation. Try to be out in nature away from people. Do at least one three-day fast if that is appropriate to your state of health.

As you pull away from all that you hold dear, your personality will change. You will be able to dedicate your life anew and create a stronger congruence to the infinite Life Force within you. Your mission or life quest will become clear and many of your cherished beliefs will fall away. You will become a freer individual and you will enjoy your new freedom.

In simplifying my life, I step beyond confusion. In clarity I express power.

By consciously changing your way of life and choosing simplicity, you will be free from confusion. The thought affirmations you create will begin to have power. They will not be cluttered by your old allegiances. They will arise instead from your clarity and sense of purpose. Your affirmations will give you courage.

You will be able to transform, create and inspire consciousness all around you.

Another way that thought forms are empowered is by concentration, and this divides into the two sub-categories of consistency and density.

Let us look at concentration generally. This is the ability you have to become what it is you want to become. As discussed briefly in an earlier chapter, the God Force does not have an opinion about your life. It just serves to empower you. To get what you want you have to be clear about it and you have to hold that thought form until your desire is granted. That is concentration.

So often we let life bump us off course. We set out on a path and almost instantly our emotions distract us or something happens and we drift off course. If you want things out of life you will have to concentrate on them, and you have to go for what you want regardless of your current situation. If you concentrate on your goal and do not get distracted, you place an additional force at your disposal. For the power of will allows you to be moved into the right place at the right time. If you do not know what you want in life, you express that uncertainty into the Universal Law. And it—being impartial—expresses back to you the same feeling. The result is that nothing flows and all your attempts to materialize your dreams fade or break up.

If you do not know what you truly want, then the best move is to begin to clear out all of those things that you know you definitely no longer want—debilitating relationships, unhelpful habits, lack of action, imbalance of one kind or another. Sooner or later what you want will become clear and then you can head toward it. The Path of Power calls for a certain aggression, as does nature. The animal in the forest goes for what he wants, and in doing so he expends energy in getting his needs met. You should adopt the same style. Lock on to what you want and go for it no matter how long it takes and you will have added concentration to your battery of techniques for self-empowerment.

A sub-division of concentration is consistency. This is simply the process of layering your intention, one thought over the next, from day-to-day until your need is met. The only trick to consistency is that you do not lace it with negative yearning. This pushes your intention away. Once you decide what you want, then think about it from time to time, feel it granted. But be careful. If you pine for something you will never have it and even if you should get what you want, it will be distasteful to you. By keeping emotion out of your intention, by detaching from the result, you allow energy to flow freely and things appear in your life. The balance is subtle. But then life is subtle, is it not?

The difficulty is that the mind does not like to concentrate. It does not do so naturally. If you have meditated, you will know how hard it is to stop thoughts from flitting through the mind. But every thought you have contributes to the Universal Law, and if you cannot control your thought pattern, you lose energy. By developing a kind of turbo-concentration, you allow the full force of your being to empower your life. Also, if you are interested in accessing the worlds through the tunnel I spoke about, you will have to practice concentration, for without it your journey is not possible. Sit still in front of a candle and see how long you can concentrate on it without letting any extraneous thoughts distract you. Once you can get to one minute, then move on to two minutes and so on. This exercise increases your ability to concentrate.

Consistency means deciding what you want and holding on to your intention until your dream is met. You must be committed to your goal even though it seems a long way off. Imagine for a moment that you want to be an architect, but you do not have enough money to pay for your college tuition. Focus! You would support your intention greatly by buying books and visiting great architectural buildings and studying on your own in the library. You would be moving toward your goal even if you do not have the money at this time to materialize your dream. By concentrating on what is in front of you, rather than the total picture, you eventually get what you want.

To get to the next space, to your goal, you have to travel through the one you are in. It is almost as if the thoughts you usually have must be used up or worn out before you can make changes. How often have you affirmed a new intention and found yourself bogged down in old patterns? This is because the old ways are tough to dismiss. It takes patience. That is why the great dramas of your life are useful. Dramatic events have a way of clearing the path of debris. After such experience you may feel lost and exhausted and beat up because your ego has taken a royal bashing and was forced to retreat. But in the wake of the drama a space occurs which allows new understanding to filter in and growth to occur.

Your thoughts are stacked around you. Some are very intense, others are more whimsical. As we look at the density or validity of thoughts we can see that some of them have greater density than others. The density is basically empowered by will and emotion as expressed through personal power. The greater the intensity, the stronger the thought.

Desire or need is the strongest factor contributing to the intensity of your thoughts. You will usually have thoughts that express needs.

When you have a *genuine* need the Universal Law has a way of delivering it to you. This is not because the Law wants to help you, it is because your thought is empowered by your will. How many times in your life have you found yourself in a desperate situation and something or someone has come along unexpectedly to save you in the nick of time. Why?

Is this God's way of helping the stragglers? No, the explanation is more complex. For example, if you have not eaten for three days, the mind, and especially the ego, become perturbed. Your personality believes that perhaps you will die. Your hunger becomes an intense need. The intensity of that need pervades your entire consciousness. You are not thinking about what movies are playing at the local theater, you are thinking about survival. That need is so strong that its density acts like a magnet: it pulls very strongly from the physical plane for a solution to its need.

If you are walking in a big city, the chance that you will get or be given food is very strong. If, on the other hand, you are an astronaut on the moon and the folks back home forgot to pack your lunch, then you exist in a dimension where there is no congruence to your thought form so your need cannot be met. (You become real thin!)

In developing your affirmations it will be important for you to place yourself, not just your consciousness, in the appropriate location for your need to be fulfilled. If you are a real estate agent and you need to sell houses each month in order to eat, you have to be near the marketplace. If you hide yourself in a mountain cave, putting out goodly affirmations of thought, you will get nowhere. Concerted action in the marketplace is the key. If you just cast your fate to the wind you will get blown around a lot.

Your affirmations of thought will enable you to find real solutions to your needs, but the easiest thing to fulfill is a need. Often, the ego will confuse needs with desires. It is not impossible to materialize a desire, but needs are easier. Once you have all your needs met then you can expand to your desires. Remember that the God Force does not quantify how much you can have, nor does it differentiate between needs and desires. Only man does that. Only man has "poverty consciousness." The God Force does not recognize poverty, for if it did it would have to *be* poverty, and it is not. It is abundance.

Have you ever wondered why so many people think poverty is spiritual, or Godlike? Why they endorse and honor it? Why they tolerate it? They do so because a part of their consciousness has not gone beyond it. The mind endorses poverty as a necessary evil and then tries to profit from the situation. Accepting poverty allows the mind to play "poor me." Being poor allows us to garner sympathy by using emotion to manipulate others into reacting. The poor receive so much attention and media coverage because the energy draws others into the familiar negative emotions associated with want.

A poor person reduces his expectations and efforts and rationalizes accepting less from himself. He claims, "I live in squalor because I am poor." The truth is, "I am poor so I live in squalor."

Poverty then becomes a misfortune, something you catch, like a disease—not the result of a lack of concerted action. In fact, poverty is often a learned response. Most people who are poor create it for themselves, for you cannot be poor for long without endorsing the idea and actually becoming fairly comfortable with it. If a person likes his poverty why would another intrude on that and try to change it? But we do. And conversely, we invent systems that endow people with poverty.

Let me explain. These concepts apply to poverty found in Western societies, not to the kind of poverty found in Africa which has a different spiritual evolution. In our society, if there were no dole, welfare or food stamps, poverty would shrink to almost nothing. Feeding the hungry removes the incentive the poor have to fix their dilemma. When a poor person says, "I need to eat," his resolve and hence his affirmation is weak since he knows he can always go to the soup kitchen as a last resort. He feels no real urgency. He may fall further into apathy and say, "This is my destiny, there is no way out." and so find none. The cycle for settling for less and receiving less spins around and around.

The poor teach their children lessons from their own experience. So you develop a society in which a part of the populace lives permanently on the handouts of others. And because the handout is offered by the government, there is little emotion or gratitude involved in accepting the gift. Eventually a class arises that lives permanently on welfare. They demand it as their right and it becomes a pension which they receive from society to supplement the income they often receive from secretly working. As you read the newspaper and see all the help wanted ads you may wonder why there is so much unemployment. But if a man does not have to work to survive, why would he do so?

The concept of shifting the responsibility for providing for oneself to someone else is handed down from generation to generation and families stay on welfare for years. But the true ghetto is of the mind. Weakness becomes an acceptable disease which is difficult to overcome. That disease is endemic to the

Western societies which have bloated "social security" systems.

Holland is a good example. They have a massive social security structure that is paid for by the working people through some of the highest personal taxation rates in the world. In the space of one generation the Dutch have gone from being a proud nation of farmers, merchants and traders to a bankrupt nation with a massive drug problem and the largest 'hippy' population in the world.

In these societies it is as though the populace existed at the bottom of a well, the walls of which are created by an apathy so deep it is almost impossible for any individual to escape. We each find ourselves in various forms of the same dilemma. Our situation may not be quite as bleak, but the same principles are at work. In childhood, each of us accepted the beliefs of others; regardless of whether those beliefs were strong or weak, we live by them. To overcome that takes great courage and sometimes we risk loneliness as we drift away from our old friends and beliefs.

Spiritual growth provides the experience of constant change. It means leaving the old and preparing to accept the new. As you develop the courage to become truly independent you will find that the Universal Law supports you. You are like the lone sailor crossing the high seas, who receives an energy boost by the sheer courage of his attempt. No one will necessarily thank you or say, "Jolly good effort, Harry," but your courage will further your feeling of expectancy, of the Life Force, of honest endeavor.

As your life grows more intense you will achieve things you never dreamed possible. But if you have to wait for circumstances around you to be just right, you will place your goals in a "future-self mode" and the Universal Law which is in the permanent "now", will not respond. You must begin where you are with whatever you have, and move step by step with patience toward your goal. The excitement of being on the path and of building your independence empowers you. Things have a way of working out, and you eventually reach wherever you are going.

By living in the present I acknowledge truth in my life. That strengthens me.

Some people might say that surely not everyone can be independent. You must have social movements, governments, unions, armies, as well as rules, regulations, laws, do's and don'ts. If not, how would the trains run? They have a point.

In the world today there are billions of people at various stages of personal and spiritual evolution. Everyone has different needs and different lessons to learn. Each of us has a spiritual goal on the earth plane, even if that spiritual goal is unattractive or dismal to others. To the Higher Self everything has some value and certain events have great value. Look at it like this: some people get to go to the Super Bowl and they get to sit in the best seats and enjoy the game in comfort and luxury, while others attend in cheaper seats and still others are selling peanuts or cleaning the toilets—but everyone gets to experience the game. The physical plane is a place where we collect experiences, nothing more.

Some people are not here to be free. That is not what they need and they would be insecure in total freedom. For example, look at Russia following the Communist Revolution. In the first few years millions of people escaped, but millions more did not. In fact, many returned having found the relative freedom of the West extremely taxing.

Not everyone needs freedom. Rather, most people need restriction for at least a part of their lives. When they are restricted they learn about themselves. Once they have strengthened themselves somewhat they are then ready to go beyond their restrictions and taste freedom.

But, for all those that walk away to true freedom there are many more who embrace restriction. These are the people who drive the trains. Still there is no high or low, there is only gradual unfoldment. One Person may be slightly more unfolded than another, but both have the God Force within them, both have the potential to set themselves free. The needs of one Higher Self are no more important than the needs of another.

It is man's tendency, once he accepts God, to feel that somehow that acceptance of God makes him better than his fellow man. So sometimes Jews think they are better than Moslems, Moslems think themselves better than Jews or Catholics, who in turn feel more annointed than Protestants. And if you look at the "New Age" or the "Self Realization" movement you will find people who believe they are part of a metaphysical aristocracy and that all Southern Baptists, Methodists, or Catholics are unconscious louts. To them the only way to experience the God Force is through the enlightened teachings of Swami Rami the Barmy.

It is difficult to avoid this hypocrisy, for we come to God through the ego and the ego is attached to its holier-than-thou attitudes. We feel that we are slightly higher than others, that people should treat us in some special way simply because we are so enlightened, so aware, so far ahead.

It is possible to go beyond the ego's pettiness. One must first allow people to be where they are and second, not judge them. The truly spiritual person has developed within himself the power to be magnanimous. The power to say, "I am responsible for myself and I do the best I can. I love myself and I love others. But I cannot be responsible for them. The way they live their life is a part of their evolution. I cannot know their needs and so I do not judge them or make comment. If you ask me what I think, I will say that I do not think, for I genuinely do not know. I am only just now becoming aware of my spiritual needs—how could I be aware of the needs of others?"

Once you can attain that consciousness you will disengage from others and become a true individual. If others are drawn to you and to what you have to say, that is well and good. If they are not, well that is fine too. Everyone is in the right place at the right time.

In developing your affirmations, you will use energy, Life

Force, concentration, and intensity. When power comes to you the ego may be seduced by the sudden attention and you may fall victim to a feeling of righteousness. There is nothing more unpleasant than a person who is always "right." They often are determined to force that "righteousness" upon others—and end by imprisoning those they would save. When you discover the true meaning of life you will walk away and let others discover it in their own time.

We will look next at aspects of space and time in relation to consciousness. Our minds exist in space and time but our *inner self* does not. What might seem to be urgent to the mind is not necessarily urgent to the Higher Self. Consciousness is a part of everything around you. Your thoughts, your body, the physical environment, the dimension you exist in, your home, the things you do, are all imbued with consciousness. When you think something, it is real. It exists in a dimension of space and time that differs from the one you exist in—the one that your mind exists in.

The relationship between your thoughts and the continuum of space and time that you exist in affects everything you do. First, all the thoughts you have exist in the eternal present. You may think about a future event but it is not the event. Here is an example: You may have a daydream about meeting a friend after work and you see yourself sitting in a restaurant having coffee with that person. You feel good, but this is not reality—just a painting in consciousness *about* reality. In fact, on the day in question perhaps your friend turned up late and the restaurant was full and so you went to the movies instead.

This relationship between your thoughts and the material world is vital. For example, in order for there to be time there has to be a mind to perceive it. Outside the mind, time may be different, or non-existent. In other words, reality has to have a consciousness perceiving it in order for it to become real. A green tree in a forest is not a green tree in a forest unless there is a mind to perceive that tree. If there is no one there, it ceases to be a "tree" and it becomes a mass of molecules evolving in a dimension of nature apart from ours. How is this so? Because if a dog saw the tree it would not be a green tree, but a colorless form (because dogs are color blind.) As Einstein said, "All is relative." So there are as many trees as there are people to behold the tree. There is a famous Zen koan that asks, "Does a tree make a noise when it falls in the forest and no one is there?" The answer is a definitive *no*.

And so it is with time. There is no time beyond the consciousness of mind. A day is a measure of consciousness. If there were no people you would not have any days. Time is created by the mind, for the mind. So your thoughts and especially your affirmations, exist in the illusionary context of time. Your thought is an eternal event, even if the thought dissipates and becomes something else.

Your position in time and space in relation to your thought is vital. Your affirmations will have to materialize in the future, even if the future is only five minutes away. The thoughts you create are either about your past, the present or the future. However, even if you think about the future, it is not the "future," it is the present inventing a possible future. Now is the only reality.

If your thought form has a future characteristic then it has weakness for within the future characteristic, there has to be an element of fantasy. Even if it does not have fantasy, it will at least have some areas that are undefined. You are where your consciousness is. If your consciousness is focused on the future, your ability to change reality, which rests in the now, is lessened.

To keep your affirmation in the eternal present, you have to believe its truth, even if you do not as yet have your need met. By concentrating on the moment, cutting out all unnecessary distraction, you will feel the full strength of your power and the Universal Law will motivate and enliven you.

The mind gets bogged down by its expectations. It decides when or where something is to happen and then becomes frustrated if things do not work out. Yet all of life is guesswork. The mind extrapolates from past experience and assumes that future events will conform to that pattern. But life often presents us with different circumstances. When something unexpected happens, do not punish yourself. It is impossible to guess right all the time. The animals in the forest do not worry over what will happen, they just live life. Once you accept things as they come, and stop putting pressure on yourself, your life will grow calm. In that calm your power will grow.

Finally, as you create affirmations allow them to be free-reigning, grant them fluidity. If you try to put an affirmation into a time-frame that is too tight, the urgency you create destroys your intention. It is best to create a well-defined intention and to place it in as large and undefined a time-frame as possible. That will work. Also, watch how you define your needs when expressing affirmations. If you are not precise and your affirmation is ill-defined, it loses power. For example, "Within three months I will be richer" is an affirmation that has a comfortable time-frame, but what do you mean by richer? You could pick up a penny in the street and your wish would be granted. But was that what you meant?

By defining your thought without making it too rigid you gain density and power. So you would affirm, "Within three months I will increase my income by at least twenty percent." This affirmation has good definition, a comfortable time-frame, and it is loose enough to allow the money to come from anywhere. You have honed your thought-form into a concentrated beam of consciousness. Your wish is granted.

By being centered and concentrating on my life I quicken my evolution.

9
NIGHT AFFIRMATION THROUGH THE TUNNEL OF LIGHT

Before we conclude the section on thought affirmations, I would like briefly to discuss some of my experiments with affirmations at night. I can offer you techniques that have been invaluable to me, ideas that I feel work.

First, let us review the metaphysical background of these concepts. Man is basically a collection of consciousness, an individual molecule of the God Force. He exists in a sea of consciousness, or the physical plane. This plane has the illusion of solidity but is actually another form of the same consciousness embodied by man. It only appears solid because of the speed at which atoms move. In fact the physical plane is not solid: the atoms and molecules that appear as solid objects are basically wave-motion.

Your body is also wave-motion. But at the same time, a part of your consciousness exists at a higher level, as is a part of the Higher Self. The Higher Self is an individualized molecule of the God Force that has identity and connects you to all things. But this does not give you total knowledge.

The brain acts as an inhibitor, cutting us off from the inner dimensions of consciousness beyond the earth plane. Without this function, we would not be able to concentrate on our survival. The Higher Self is constantly with us, but it does not regulate our thought or life events. Its energy supports us and in turn we collect experiences for it. Somehow that helps it to expand.

When we are awake the ego dominates. We concentrate on our physical existence, putting aside our metaphysical self. In sleep the mind reorganizes itself, reviewing and collating, sifting the days events. Once this is complete the *inner self* can drift out of the physical plane into another dimension of existence. Because the energy of these other planes is so much more rarified than ours, the symbols used there seem foreign to us. Whatever transfer of information occurs transcends the intellect, so upon waking we have only a vague memory, a feeling, perhaps, of having been somewhere else for a few hours, a feeling of mystery — of being connected to other worlds. Sometimes we have strange dreams which seem to comment upon our life. I believe that dreams are the mind's way of translating symbols from higher worlds into a language it understands.

That communication is made from these higher worlds at night cannot be proved. But many have such experiences and believe them to be true. It is my conclusion that you could not "dream" about those worlds if a part of you did not already exist there in some form.

One day in my theta meditation, there appeared a hand which offered a strange geometric shape. It was not like anything I had seen before. It was oblong, square and triangular all rolled into one. It seemed to contain both space and time, and through it ran diagonal lines. The shape and the hand were alive with energy. The lines were a part of the symbol and it in turn belonged to the lines in some way. I later discovered it was a type of "access code" to another world, much like the digit on a computer that we press to access a file or a string of information. The symbol belonged to the being or energy I came to call the "doorkeeper." I do not know if the mysterious shape is the doorkeeper, or if it is just a symbol that represents the doorkeeper. Shortly after this experience the symbol changed and simplified itself into the shape of a wheel.

Each day I would enter a trance, and as soon as I was relaxed, the wheel would appear. Never once, in over two thousand meditations, has it ever appeared the same. It constantly changes. The shape and size of the wheel and especially the angle at which I view it, always vary. Occasionally there is more than one wheel. Once the "access code" is given, information appears in the form of symbols or sometimes words. On some occasions the tube appears which allows me to enter into other evolutions. I have noticed that the tube tends to curve to the right like a bent hose and it turns clockwise. At first I thought this was due to my being in the northern hemisphere. But on a recent trip to Australia I discovered that it turns clockwise there also.

There is a wave of energy coming down the tube and another energy going up. The two energies wrap around each other like licorice sticks. Their helix shape looks exactly like diagrams of a DNA molecule. At first I thought the tube was independent of the two energies, but then I realized that the tube or tunnel is created by the shape of the energies as they wrap around each other, and it seems to me that the tube is the area in the center of the two energy waves. *

If you have ever read accounts of people who have had near-death experiences, you will recall that many report going up a tunnel or tube. I believe the tube I see is the same and that it connects to other worlds, much like a freeway. On an early excursion up the tube, for example, I came upon a gray, "twilight world." The people there were confused and my presence terrified them. Their condition was so pitiful and I wanted to help them, but I did not know how. My efforts only caused them to become even more terrified. Every night for a week I found myself in their world. My presence was an intrusion on them and their reaction bothered me deeply. I gave up my daily trances for the month, and when I returned to my practice the twilit world was gone.

On one occasion I found myself on the threshold of an exquisitely beautiful world. It was lit by the light of God and its intensity was such as I have never seen before. I wanted to enter, and yet my energy could not sustain it. So I asked for help. A ball of white light appeared behind my left shoulder, hovered for a moment and then shot forward into that world, much like a baseball heading for the plate. Then it disappeared. It seemed that a part of me was in the ball and that when the ball entered that world it took a part of me with it. Somehow that action showed me that I could enter at a later date. What I learned from the experience is that often we forget to ask for help. We feel alone and abandoned, and yet within us there are forces that we direct, or that are directed for us perhaps by the Higher Self, just behind the mind.

As humans we wrap ourselves in our own lives and thoughts. Our minds create constant chatter. The inner worlds that would inspire us cannot communicate through that chatter. But if we turn and face that light, the power therein streams forth to meet us. At night I developed the habit of saying an affirmation of dedication which is written below. Then I review the day, starting with the most recent events, because they are closer and more intense than the events that took place at dawn, hours earlier. I am especially careful to release any feelings I have about the day, good or bad. I also review all the interactions I had with people. They seem to impact the psyche more powerfully than mundane events. I believe that reviewing the day in your mind alleviates some of the need to dream, allowing you more time to experience higher worlds during sleep. I then look at what I have learned in the day and give thanks for the exhilaration I experienced. Next, I "reach out" through the top of my head, extending my thought for as long as possible. For some reason this is very difficult. But I do it as best I can. To complete the night exercises I use an affirmation dedicating my night to service, if that is appropriate, and I call upon my Higher Self to assist me in my evolution.

I dedicate this night to service, if that is appropriate. — I call upon my Higher Self to assist me in my understanding and evolution.

On occasion I wake up in the morning with the distinct feeling of having been instructed in some way. About once every three months, I wake up in a state of celestial ecstasy. My whole being is calm and understands the meaning of things. I try to sustain

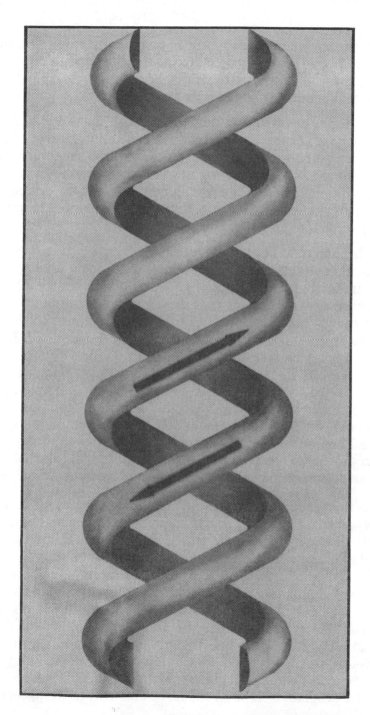

The Helix Tunnel That Joins Two Worlds

that special feeling for as long as possible by entering a light meditation. I am convinced that using the "dream time" has helped me over the years, so I suggest that you try it, for if you think about it, what else *is* there to do in the dead of the night?

At the time of this writing I have been up the tube about two hundred times. It's a place that seems to link many different worlds. When I see the tube I put out a thought to the door-keeper to show me something new. I do not seem to have much control over what occurs next. Sometimes the tube disappears. Other times I find myself in new dimensions with languages that are so foreign I have had to leave out of fear.

There seem to be as many worlds as there are human moods, and other worlds that are not human at all. Some are dreadful. For instance, there is a dimension that permeates the physical which consists of beings that are partly in the physical plane but mostly not. These beings have very gross human desires. I have seen some that look more or less human and I have seen others that seem part human, part animal. To look upon them revolts the senses. It makes me wonder what we must look like to angels. A human being is usually protected from these grosser worlds by a shield that emanates from the atoms and molecules of the body and the Life Force of the mind. The Theosophist calls this shield the etheric web. Sometimes that protection breaks down. Sometimes drugs and alcohol break it down, sometimes sickness or extreme emotional imbalance.

A man called me from New York who complained of being homosexually raped by one of these beings. The man said that while it was happening he sensed the presence of intense evil, and after the event occurred his apartment took on a repulsive odor. It seemed that this man had had an industrial accident some years before. He was on a disability pension and lived alone. Doing nothing with his life, he had allowed his stock of Life Force to fall. I believe he drank, though he denied that to me. Over the years his strength whittled away, so that the quasi-physical being could do with him what it willed. I suggested to the man a vigorous regimen of exercise and diet. And I gave him a program to rebuild his Life Force and to strengthen his alignment to the light. His life improved, and eventually he stopped calling.

From my journeys "up the tube" I have discovered fragments of knowledge that underlie the basic principles of life. But each time I visit those worlds I find that I can only glimpse at what is going on. It is like watching a film in which one is granted only a 10-second clip every half hour. From the high-speed clips one has to extrapolate what the story is.

As far as I can tell, the dimensions beyond the earth plane are divided by barriers of consciousness. The inhabitants of one world are usually unaware of the inhabitants of the others. The more rarified dimensions are permeated by the light of the God Force and seem positive and pleasing. Other worlds are gray or very dark and seem to exist solely for the sake of repressions or evil. It seems to me that the quality of the worlds is determined by their inhabitants.

As like-minded inhabitants in the dark areas become aligned, the energy they create seems to act as a trap. Their ability to entrap and bind themselves and others is fearsome. I have never discovered a way to pierce the consciousness of the dark people. They live unto themselves and they delight in the evil of their own dimension. The world today is similiar. No one sees their environment as ugly. We all consider our lives to be worthwhile, and we view our acts as good or meaningful.

Wrapped up as we are in our own thoughts, it is hard for us to step out of ourselves and really look at our lives. The thirty-day exercise mentioned earlier can help here. It allows us to see what we have become. The beauty stands out and the gray parts, if any, lie in contrast beside it.

Emmanuel Swedenborg reported that beings from one dimension could not communicate to beings of another except through the mind of the recipient. This bothered me, for I believed in spiritual mediumship and the possibility of receiving information from higher beings that is foreign to one's own consciousness. The answer turned out to be infinitely more complex than I had imagined.

Those entities that exist in the higher planes communicate directly through thoughts or feelings. They take the Life Force, mold that light to their own identity and project it. This information transfer is almost instantaneous and seems to reflect the intensity or power of the being. I believe those quantums of communication move faster than the speed of light. If I ask you to think of the sun it will take you about one half of one second to pull the image from your subconscious mind. Yet the light from the sun takes several minutes to reach us. Which leads me to speculate that our consciousness is more agile than light.

At the other end of the tube I found that if I looked at one of the symbols in the way I normally engage my eyes in the physical plane, I would lose it. It would be gone before I could register what it was. I learned to allow the symbol to impact my mind without looking at it directly. This sounds obscure, but it is not that difficult. It is mainly an exercise in getting your personality out of the way so that you can receive energy directly, in a form that is unusual but masterable. One needs a passive and accepting mind; you just do not have time to judge or analyze what you are receiving.

I surmise that the information received from the tube is understandable to anyone reaching the vibrational level in which it is created. Many of the dimensions are way beyond us so energy coming to you from a higher world has to transform itself down to the terms that are familiar to you, serving to enlighten you from within the capacity of your own consciousness, which is the only way you can really use it.

If you are familiar with channelling and spirit communication you will know that much of it is delivered in high sounding "cosmic" terms, but what is being said could be the utterances of anyone. Now I know that some may take issue with me over this point, but this is because people like to feel that some kind of White Brotherhood is delivering cosmic messages for the salvation of mankind. This helps people feel "special" and that is OK. For if the medium says, "This teaching is coming directly from the great spirit master Bongo-Dongo who died ten thousand years ago," it is more impacting than if the medium had said, "These are my teachings and though perhaps they may be inspired by Bongo-Dongo they are actually from within my own mind."

The "channel" or spirit medium does not usually have direct access to the spirit worlds with which he or she is communicating. Thus, when I say to you that the energies coming through the spirit guides are quanta of light which trigger information from within the mind of the medium, and that nothing is uttered that does not already exist there, it would be difficult for anyone who has not had a direct experience of those worlds to successfully argue the point. Further, if they had been in those inner worlds they will know that what I say is correct.

But in the end what is valuable is whether or not the teachings help people. If ol' Bongo-Dongo sets people free, then that is neat. And if you have to wrap it up in a load of "hocus-pocus" to get people to listen, who cares? The end result is what matters.

One of the aspects of Jesus' communication with the higher powers (symbolized in the Bible as his Dad) made me wonder. How is it that, if Jesus was the most cosmic being that had ever walked the earth, he did not know so many simple things—such as how electricity works, or how to ride a bike, or what to do with a rubber band? Smallpox was a curse in his time. Why could he not cure it? Now I do not mean to disparage the teachings of Jesus, but it is a valid point. I asked a friend of mine who is a priest what he thought. He replied that the Christian view is that Jesus was familiar with modern technology but that he chose not to mention it.

Maybe and maybe not. But I feel that Swedenborg was right. Jesus had to translate information coming into his consciousness from the higher powers, in terms his mind understood. So he talked about love, and the law, and respecting all things. That was what was important in his time, as it is today. The invention of the light bulb and the cure for smallpox would come with nearly two thousand years of human evolution.

Does this invalidate his teachings? Not at all. This merely confirms Swedenborg's view that we can receive only the information that is within our mind's capacity.

I believe that when Jesus was baptised by John on the bank of the Jordan River, Jesus was "drowned": the ego part of his mind was released by that event, symbolized in the Bible as the dove leaving him. Once the ego was to one side, the power of the cosmic projection that assisted him emerged. Nonetheless this projection was communicated through his mind in the context of the world to which he was accustomed.

Your mind contains vast mines of information of which, for the most part, you are unaware. Energy from higher worlds can present that information to you in a bright and fresh way. But it won't give you the cure for AIDS unless your consciousness contains the basis for the formula already. Edison did thousands of experiments before he came up with the light bulb. But the seeds of that breakthrough existed in his mind long before he became conscious of it.

In night affirmations I feel it is important that you "reach out" to receive energy that may seem to affect you in unfamiliar ways. About ten per cent of the time I have spent "up the tube", I have been in areas that are foreign to me. Because the symbols were not a part of my consciousness I could not understand what was being communicated there, but those experiences were valuable because they taught me to expand my view of the inner worlds. Every situation is made up of what you think is going on (which is bounded by your perceptions) and what is going on beyond your perceptions. The hidden meaning of life will give up its secrets gradually. With practice you will develop a sixth sense for grasping the meaning behind what seems obvious, and you will delight as more and more resources open to you.

The gradual opening process is reflected in the etheric energy shield around your body. The Hindus call the vortices of energy in that shield *chakras*. Through these vortices energy flows into and out of the shield. Interestingly, the energy flowing in and out of the *chakras* resembles the process taking place in the tube, on a smaller scale. I believe that in death your energy exits this life through the *chakras* or because of the *chakras*, which give you access to the tube.

Many who are on a spiritual path have spoken to me about a tickling sensation on the top of their heads, in the area of the *crown chakra*. Some of it may be dandruff—yet the stories are so similar that it leads me to conclude that the tickling is caused at times by the expansion and contraction of that vortex. I have had the same experience, especially in the throat area: from time to time I have felt as if there were energy pushing my chin up.

The process of expanding the *chakras* must be gradual. If the opening process is too rapid or forced, there can be damage and even physical pain. On one occasion, while in trance, I attempted a maneuver that was way beyond my capacity. I elevated myself out of my body about a foot and a half horizontally. My astral body faced the ceiling. I then turned the astral body around in a full turn so that I was face to face with my physical body, and then I attempted to lift my physical body upwards. Very tricky! In the process I felt a flash of searing pain shoot through my throat. The pain snapped me back to reality and my physical body was under great stress for about twenty minutes. This experience apparently was not so unusual. I have heard of trance mediums who communicate using the throat *chakra*, hemorrhaging internally in the throat when they were out of balance. And a British medium that I knew of vaguely, had his heart *chakra* pack up in trance and he departed for the spirit worlds on the spot, much to the consternation of those gathered.

The *chakra* system is the lifeline to the God Force and it cannot be forced to open. It has been my experience that it opens gradually over the years, as you develop as a human being. The key is to develop the magnanimity which enables you to be a part of all things without emotion. When you are emotional the heart *chakra* closes down in its own defense, like one of those aquatic anemones that shuts the instant you touch it. It does so to avoid damage to the etheric web that might be caused by the massive uncontrolled rush of energy through the *chakra*, emanating from your imbalance. As the heart *chakra* closes, it cuts you off from the Life Force and your ability to detoxify your feelings and thoughts is reduced. That is why negative people stay that way for years: the toxicity of their feelings isolates them and they live and breathe only their own reality which reinforces their decision to be negative.

The key to expanding the heart *chakra* is openness. The more you invest in softness and caring and the more you relax about your life, the more your energy flows. The techniques discussed in the earlier sections on thought empowerment will help. Let's review them: *Variance*, or the ability to accept your life in real terms, not in terms of fantasy; *Identity*, or believing yourself to be identical with the inner God Force; *Congruence*, or living your life limitlessly and developing your Life Force through a strong physical body, emotional control, mental control, and philosophical understanding. This includes having a philosophy that grants you the freedom to be an individual, free of those senseless rules and regulations we impose on ourselves.

Finally, I believe that the practice of meditation and relaxation is vital, for it allows you to review your life and to detach from the exigencies of daily life. Yoga seems to have a great benefit, as does shiatsu massage, acupuncture and other forms of self-healing. Whatever method you choose is fine as long as it works for you and as long as you practice it according to an organized system of sanctuary that allows you to be silent, to be with yourself and to review your progress.

Thought form affirmation is very much a matter of practicing and being consistent. With daily practice, old habits will gradually dissolve and the strength of the new will bring you to greater heights. Of course this takes patience. Eventually, however you will reach immortality, not just in your thoughts—but, more importantly, in your feelings. All your hopes and dreams will open to you with loving arms and you can truly say, "I am power." With your word as law that thought form resonates through a thousand celestial dimensions and something somewhere, beyond eternity, celebrates in the joy of your return.

In this day I express
love and openness to each person I meet,
for I know that I am truly loveable.

10
AFFIRMATIONS
OF HEART OR FEELING

A word is just a symbol. It does little to describe the object to which it refers. For example, the word "door" tells the listener little about the nature of the door.

The spoken word is not as strong as a current thought, and that in turn is not as strong as a feeling. In the Warrior's Wisdom five-day intensives* that I present in Taos, New Mexico, I concentrate on developing peripheral and etheric perception in the attendees by using exercises that the doorkeeper taught me as part of the Quickening. To expand your energy successfully, you first have to develop a heightened sense of feeling. This is because dimensions of consciousness are basically boundries of consciousness and are made up of feelings. What differentiates a dimension of hell from, say, heaven, is the way the denizens of that dimension feel about themselves. It is a lack of perception or feeling that creates hell. It is the Quickening that creates your ability to enter a celestial heaven.

What you think goes to create what you feel. But it is your feelings that color your reality. These philosophies that say, "What you think is what you are," are only partially right. The thoughts you express change the cloud of feeling around you and that feeling, which is personal to you, pulls from the Life Force energy that is similiar. A word describes a thought form and thought forms create feeling. But only the feelings are real, metaphysically.

Consider a relationship that you have with someone. What is real about that relationship is the feeling, negative or positive, that you have about it. If you think of a friend you have not

131

seen for some months you may find it difficult to remember their face but you will be able to recall some characteristic of how they feel to you.

Feeling is one way of describing within your consciousness the quality of ambience you are in. If I say to you the word "abundance" it may mean a thousand things to you. For example, the word may arouse in you a feeling of being looked after, of being safe, of having enough money. Or it may be the feeling of sitting at a table full of fine food or relaxing in the rear seat of a limosine. As you become more aware of the feelings that things arouse in you, you will notice that everything around you has an energy "thumbprint" that describes its intrinsic quality. The clothes you wear, the music you listen to, the people you know, the home you live in, the work you do—each goes to create the dimension or energy that you live in. But before we can look at the creation of an affirmation of feeling, we have to look at the way your thinking blocks you off from sensitivity and how, as humans in a modern age, we are not taught to develop a heightened sense of feeling.

If, say, you are concentrating on an important problem, all of your thoughts and feelings will be engaged by that problem. You become the problem. By identifying with the problem, you gradually solidify its reality around you, cutting yourself off from other energy.

As you identify with the problem your feelings become clouded, and you will find that you cannot see the forest for the trees. New energy finds no opening to refresh you. The reality around you reflects only the contours of the problem in which you are immersed. The solution must come from what you believe, since that is the only reality you can perceive at that time. The same logic applies to your life. Each event ratifies your experience and that experience settles in your consciousness like a block of concrete, every bit as real.

The feelings you generate pull you into areas of the physical plane that match those feelings and they will dictate what you will choose to do day-to-day. For example, if you enter a nightclub, your feelings have to accept the ambience of that nightclub, for you are signing up to take a bath in that energy. The club may be noisy and crowded, people may be drinking liquor, there may be flashing lights and a highly charged atmosphere of sexuality.

As you walk into that club, you make hundreds of decisions in the time it takes you to make your first three steps. Your feelings, like radar, instantly flash to all corners of the room and give you an energy reading. The five senses report what is going on at the physical level and your feelings give you a more subtle understanding. About 80 per cent of the information will be below your conscious threshold, and as you concern yourself with finding a table, your mind will be asleep to that information. But the information is there in your subconscious mind, and you can train yourself to be aware of it and to use it to your benefit.

Meanwhile, you have your five senses which will be reasonably informative. But even if you are wide awake and alert, you will only be aware of a part of your sensory input. That is because we all concentrate on what interests us, and thus we block out a large percentage of what we see, hear, and touch. This process of blocking out certain selective, subliminal information delivered by your feelings and conscious information from the five senses, is common to everyone. We are not used to picking up peripheral information. We are so often immersed in our lives that we do not see the big picture.

As you develop affirmations of feelings, you will want to work on expanding your ability to consciously receive and trust sensory information from those feelings. Feelings never lie. A person cannot hide what they feel. They can hide what they think—by saying one thing and believing another—but their feelings are clearly visible to the trained eye.

By the time you are seated at the table in the nightclub, you have asked yourself, "Does this atmosphere complement my feelings?" and you have answered, more or less, "Yes." For if the answer were no, you would leave. As you confirm your presence in that dimension of feelings called "nightclub" you become open to all the possibilities that arise from that choice, at that moment in space and time.

The energy of the Life Force flows fluidly through the physical plane because it is in all things. But in the structures of man, the Life Force is entrapped within the parameters created. It is like mist in a box, it is fluid but only within its man-made limitation. Thus in the nightclub there are probably ten thousand things you can experience, and ten billion you cannot. You can experience someone accidentally pouring a tomato juice on your best shirt, but you cannot experience the sound of a tiger fishing in a river.

So as you sit in the nightclub you begin to soak up the energy there and that will also begin to change how you feel. As the music throbs so will the neurons in your brain, oscillating in the same rhythm. When a person brushes past you, their energy and yours will mix and there will be a transfer of that energy. If they are tired and you are fresh they will pillage a portion of your Life Force.

If you are thinking sexually about the waitress and she is thinking about going to church on Sunday, she may inherit a part of your feelings and she may fantasize about sleeping with church organists. As you change to become a part of the nightclub dimension, you also change it. It is all the energy that is there, plus or minus whatever you have.

Within that block of energy are many feelings that go to make up the overall picture. Your feelings will search out similar feelings. If, for example, there are three Mafia bosses at the next table and they are full of anger, any anger in you will combine with theirs and become more acute. You may find a reason to become angry. You may turn to them and tell them to take a hike, and in turn one may respond by smashing you in the mouth. Scene two has you on the floor with a bleeding lip, watching the strobe lights flickering in the switchblade the thug holds to your nose. "It's only 10:15," you say, "a million things can happen by dawn." And so they can.

As we move through the physical plane we sign up for each dimension of feelings and the possibilities therein. We take whatever we want and we move on. Much of what you feel about life is energy you inherited from others. Once you become aware of how that affects you, you can begin to avoid situations that do not affirm your view of life. The trick is to identify what you want and what you do not want.

So often we make decisions without being aware of the most important facts. So we enter the nightclub, see a cute waitress and think, "This will be fun." But our feelings may have flashed us a message that said, "This place is very dangerous. The weirdo in the corner works for the Mafia bosses, and they are all close to leaving the earth plane, because a busload of irate Corsicans up the road plan to spread this lot all over the wallpaper on the north wall of the club."

The sage watches everything. The sage is open to receive. So as he walks into the club he disregards the advances of the waitress and pauses in silence, liberating himself from opinion and judgment. In less than three seconds he takes in the whole picture. He lets his senses travel through the scene and is aware of the actual and peripheral information available.

Once that is stored, the sage sends out a question from his heart *chakra*. The Universal Mind gives him its print-out. He sees the weirdo and notices the erratic energy he emits. The print-out reads, "drugs." The sage can see at thirty feet that the pupils in the weirdo's eyes are dilated. Then he looks at the Mafia bosses and he senses restriction and evil. From the corner of his eye he picks up a subtle movement under a table and is instantly aware that the three painted ladies and the smiling Chinamen seated there are operating a "love for hire" franchise. He observes without judgment.

The whole club vibrates with an air of expectancy. Seventeen Higher Selves, encased in their human bodies, have traveled through the night to be at that club to die. The sage looks at the change that has taken place in the crown *chakras* of the Mafia bosses and those seated at the tables nearby and he can see that at some time in the next seventy-two hours those people will depart the physical plane. Analyzing that information with everything else he senses, the sage leaves the club to buy an ice cream across the street. Sure enough, the irate Corsicans show up, park their bus at the curb and decimate the club. The driver of the bus, a swarthy little gent from Cleveland who hates gun fire, joins the sage for a double scoop of mocha chocolate. The power of the sage is such that the little man is instantly converted to a higher energy and he drives off in the bus determined to live a more genteel life. Meanwhile, his pals spill out onto the sidewalk, amazed to discover that the transportation has left without them, and even more amazed at the way the red lights of the nine police cars parked in the street reflect off the beer advertisement on the corner. The sage smiles and says to himself, "It's only 10:45, nine hundred thousand things can happen before dawn."

With affirmations of feelings or heart it would be easy just to say, "change your feelings." But it is a little more complicated than that, for first you have to be fully aware of what is going on around you so that you can make helpful corrections in your attitudes.

As you walk through life, practice becoming more aware of what is going on through your five senses. Try going into a restaurant, pausing at the door and looking over in one slow sweep. Try to pick up and retain as much information as possible. Then walk out. Have a friend ask you detailed questions about what you observed. What color dress was the African lady on the balcony wearing? How many chairs were there? What kind of carpet? And so on. Then return and see how much you got right. When you learn to concentrate and can close down your own concerns, life around becomes more thrilling, for you pick up more of it.

Each and every day I am becoming more and more sensitive to my surroundings. I am always in the right place at the right time.

If you have lived forty years and you have observed 50 per cent of what was around you, you might as well have lived for twenty. By becoming more aware, you gain a second life. Now you have two: the one you live and the one you used to miss. It's a matter of practice. In noticing life you develop extrasensory abilities, for you are telling your mind that you want it to pick up subtle information. There are many exercises and techniques you can use to develop your skill. For example, walk down a street and find two people who are talking to one another. Walk two or three yards ahead of them. Quiet the chatter in your mind and concentrate on listening to their conversation. Practice hearing "out of the back of your head." If you can pick up their conversation clearly, increase your step so that now you are five or six yards ahead of them, then increase your awareness to accommodate their voices' lower volume. Pull all of your attention into what is being said, and try to remember every detail. As you listen, watch those who pass and remember every detail about them too. Next, concentrate on the smells in the street, and without moving your head, locate the sources of those smells. The perfume worn by a woman, the hamburger stand, the exhaust fumes, and so on. You now have an acute awareness of your surroundings in terms of sight, sound and smell. Add the sense of touch. Use the clothes you are wearing for this. Become aware of how they feel as you walk. Then buy something to eat and engage your sense of taste. Once you have mastered concentration on all of your senses at once, you will have mastered the first step.

For step two you must begin to pick up the peripheral information of the street and become aware of what is in the corner of your eye. The cells of your eyes are made up of rods and cones. The cones are in the center of the eye and the rods, which are more sensitive, are to the side. So even though your peripheral awareness is not as detailed as your direct vision, the rods are able to pick up subtle or etheric energy that is not available to the cones. If you want to learn how to "see" more you will have to become more aware of the latent visual capacity you have. To assist your peripheral vision, concentrate on it habitually until it comes naturally. I have noticed that peripheral awareness increases when a person is tired. This is a combination of eye muscle fatigue and the slowing process of the brain. So your best time for developing peripheral vision will be at night, or any time when you are tired.

Now you are ready to add step three, which involves opening yourself to all of the subliminal information around you. Begin by opening to people. When someone walks towards you, close your eyes slightly and look beyond them over their left shoulder. As they approach, concentrate on their center chest area (their heart *chakra*) and, without judging, try to discern information about their life that comes to you from your feelings. Your first impressions will be accurate. Do not think about the person; your mind will lead you astray. Then look at them directly—I mean really look. Look at their weight and height, the way they walk, how they carry themselves, the condition of their fingernails, the clothes they wear, are they tailored or slung together? Is the person clean or dirty, dressed expensively or cheaply? Now see if the visual information confirms your feelings.

A person's face and body reflect his or her overall feeling about life. When a person talks, listen to every word they say and become aware of the spaces or pauses between their words. There is usually more true information in their silences than in their conversation. While they talk watch the movement of their eyes and eye muscles, the muscles of their jaw, the movements of their hands. Remember that it takes about half a second for a feeling within the subconscious to permeate the conscious body, so their facial reactions will lag ever so slightly behind what they are saying.

Their feelings will be signaled to you. The slightest change in their expression, even if they are trying to hide something from you, will be apparent. Watch their eyes, and notice their pupils. Are they dilated? If they feel good aboutyou or if they are stoned, their pupils will widen. If they are worried or afraid their pupils will close. If they are uncomfortable they will look away. It may be only a slight eye movement but it will not escape your notice.

Watch how their body shifts as they talk. Are their arms or legs crossed? Do they face you or sit at an angle? Do they touch you when they talk, and how do they react if you touch them? Touch them and find out. Each person will communicate out of their persona or the image they have of themselves and the image of themselves they want you to accept. Their intellect will spin you the official story but their feelings will give you the truth.

The process of expanding your heart's self-awareness is the key to understanding your own inner personality. Everyone feels but most of those feelings lie underground. By becoming sensitive to another's subtle messages you will learn about your own subtle energies. In doing so you will be able to identify what it is that you put out into the Universal Law, and that is the first step to change — knowing yourself.

The techniques of searching for the "feeling" of things is a learned habit. Eventually, it comes to you naturally. Here is another exercise you can use. Most four-color magazines carry complex advertisements for liquor. The ads cost a fortune, sometimes as much as forty to fifty thousand dollars a page. The advertisers know that they have only one and one half seconds to engage your attention. To do so, they airbrush naked bodies in various subliminal erotic poses into their photography. They know that the *inner you* will respond.

Creating an emotional response has more impact than giving the reader information or slogans. An ad that says, "Drink this whiskey," is fifty grand down the drain, but if they can get you to respond sexually or if they can scare you, they will have created the desired effect. We often drink when we are nervous, do we not? And we associate drinking with loss of sexual inhibition.

To use these subliminals as an exercise to enhance feeling, first put yourself in a relaxed state. Turn the pages of the magazine slowly until you come upon one of the four-color liquor ads. Cast your eye over the advertisement and notice where your feelings are attracted. There may be more than one area as ads often contain twenty or more subliminal prompts. By carefully scrutinizing the parts of the ad that attract your feelings, you will become aware of the subliminal hanky-panky. You may have to turn the page around somewhat, but you will soon get it. There will be bodies or parts of bodies in the ice cubes or in the condensation on the bottle. Next, look for the fear prompts. They will usually take the form of ghouls, skulls or tombstones.

As you uncover the hidden parts of life, your suppressed feelings come to the surface. You will discover who you really are. With courage your life will change overnight. Becoming real is only a matter of making up your mind to do so. You no longer have to defend yourself, make excuses to others, or try to please them. You are an immortal child of the universe. What you are is what you are.

Start to identify what you really feel. Make a list of the main headings of your life. In the left column write down the following:

Where you live.

Whom you live with (enter their individual names, especially people who are meaningful to you, such as your spouse, lover, children or boss.)

How you make your living.

What you do with it (shelter, food, obligations.)

What creative endeavors you are involved in.

Your feeling about life (Is it in or out of control?)

The condition of your body.

Other major factors in your life.

Next to each heading, write one of the following feelings:

Satisfactory

Not Satisfactory

Supportive

Not Supportive

Pleasing

Not Pleasing

Strong

Weak

If these words do not describe your exact feelings, then enter your own word.

You are examining these situations in order to design a life that is free of struggle and emotional upheaval, one that includes love, pleasure and total fulfillment, one that will nurture you. Basically you are going to plug into your life a "struggle-o-meter" to discover how much life nurtures you and how much does not.

As you get your reading from the struggle-o-meter it is soon obvious what areas need change and what will help you to feel free and refreshed as an individual.

In the third column, write next to each category how you would improve a good situation or resolve a bad one. For example, if you have a job that you hate, write a word about what action you will take to fix this situation. This may involve talking to your colleagues or boss, or it may involve plans to hightail it out of there.

By analyzing your life you can observe what supports you and what does not. You are free to alter or improve anything. It took you a while to get into these situations and it may take a while to unravel them all, but you are patient. Situations cannot change until your feelings about them change.

Next, what about money? Without money you are sunk as a spiritual being unless you are willing to disappear up a mountain top. But "dropping out" won't really work; today's game is "involvement." The trick is to take the energy you have developed and use it to make something of yourself and your life. Do you avoid handling your finances, using the excuse that spiritual growth puts you "above" the need for money? In this era there is more communication, art, creativity, healing, and travel available than at any other time. It would be a shame if you missed out on all that. This is your one chance to take in all the experiences you can. If this were not a part of your Higher Self's intention you would not have bothered to be here at this time.

Developing abundance involves effort. But there is a big difference between effort and struggle. If you are doing work just to survive it becomes drudgery, which pillages your energy. Decide what you want, and begin to go for it—right now. Getting paid for what you love to do is one of life's great joys. It is a way of honoring yourself.

Money is your escape hatch, but that escape hatch is not effective until you work for yourself. No matter how considerate your boss is you always live according to his destiny, not yours. This is fine for a time but eventually you will have to   into complete control. If it is not possible for you to be self-employed then begin by developing as much freedom you can within your employment. Perhaps, you can sell your expertise to your employer as a subcontractor.

Alternatively, you should try to develop other income producing ideas, or part time work or investments, so that you have as many options as possible. This grants you fluidity and allows you to be adaptable. You could move at an instant if you wished.

For some, adaptability is natural, but not for others. Yet often it is impossible for you to become a success if you do not leave the place where you were raised, for it holds you in a vice grip of memories and associations. It is hard to affirm, "I am this now," when everyone around you remembers and affirms the old image of you. Leaving a safe haven and heading out is an affirmation in itself that says, "I now have the power. My positivity and effort will guarantee my success no matter where I go or what I choose to do."

Likewise, developing and sustaining an affirmation of feeling means pressing up against your last known boundary and obliterating it with the force of your will. You emerge as a heroic being, beyond uncertainty and with a mastery of life. After that, what is death but another coming and going? Once you have reached that peak, fear melts away with the intensity of the light. You have completed your goal in life and anything else you experience is an extra gift to be savored. The path well-traveled is the goal—not the destination reached.

As you reach this peak in your feeling, that, in itself, becomes an affirmation. You view your life and the lives of others as a kindly observer would rather than as an emotional participant.

Some years ago I had a girlfriend who had a serious drug problem. Her habit caused me endless concern and worry. Though I did not condone her habit I did not condemn it either. That would have only reiterated the attitude of her family and society, her response to which caused her addiction in the first place. So I took it upon myself to support her. I trotted endlessly through the night, talking to a host of sleazy characters, helping her to stay safe while she bought her drugs. I came to understand the complexity of drug addiction and I felt compassion for her.

One day, crying, she asked me where I thought it would all lead. I told her in truth that she would die, and soon. That got her attention, and she slowly began the healing process. At that time in England you could register with the Ministry of Health as a drug user. They issued you an identity card, affectionately known as the NUJ card (The National Union of Junkies.) She registered. This was the first step in her recovery. Until that time she would not admit she had a problem. Eventually, despite her acceptance of her disease, I decided it was best for us to stop being together, even though I thought at the time that she would surely die. But a few years later she was cured and had married and settled down in the Mediterranean. Everything worked out fine. Her seminar in "daily life" had cost her $40,000, but she had gotten the message.

Sometimes letting people go is the best thing you can do for them. You cannot coerce them into being sensible. Sometimes they need to experience degradation and failure before they can come to success.

In conclusion, let us review some of the main points about affirmations of feelings or heart. First you have to develop a sensitivity to the world around you. Then you must look honestly at your life, analyze how you feel about it, and determine what steps you should take to improve whatever is unsatisfactory.

When you experience mood swings, as we all do, watch carefully when your feelings begin to deteriorate and immediately correct them. If you know that you become grumpy when tired then you should avoid having to make decisions when in that state. If a certain person causes you imbalance, release them from your life. It is so easy to say to someone, "I honor your decision to be who you are, but I would prefer if you took it elsewhere."

The world around you is out of balance and its "Tick-tock" will tend to pull you down. As you learn to detach, things will cease to affect you. You will also find it helpful to reduce the amount of absolute contact you have with the world. Avoid crowds. Keep your special view of the world unto yourself. Your destiny is separate because you are one of those rare people who has the mastery of his or her life. I feel it is important to be informed about what is going on in the world, but be careful not to be pulled in emotionally. Stay away from world "causes," they are ego traps. If you want to love the world, save it and feed it, that's great. But first, love and feed yourself. Then, love, feed and support those close to you. If you have spare time, you can march with your banner. But do not crusade in lieu of becoming powerful. You can help others when they ask for it, but not before.

Finally, you will develop "mystery," and from secrecy you gain power. When people know all about you, they cast hooks into your energy, like pirates attacking a ship, and it becomes infinitely more difficult to "detach." Also, as you move through life, grant yourself patience. Given the many years it has taken you to evolve into your current pattern, it will take a few years to work your way out of it.

Whatever weaknesses you have—weaknesses of character, of lifestyle, of circumstance—they are beautiful. They allow you to learn and go on to higher things. If your life were perfect you would die, for there would be no reason for your Higher Self to be here. Have compassion for yourself and understand that in all imbalance there is strength, and that there is no perfection, no absolute completion. Everything in life is a part of the "quest." If the goal or the quest were attainable the world would end. It is the path well-trod that makes you heroic, not the end result.

My life is heroic.
I acknowledge and honor each step I take.

11
AFFIRMATIONS
OF ESSENCE OR ACTION

Affirmations of essence or action speak louder than words. There is nothing like affirming, "I feel abundant," with $50,000 in cash on the kitchen table. Somehow the mind gets it readily.

The process of creating action to support your affirmation is not complicated. Each day you have many successes. To you they may seem unimportant. But to the sage everything is important.

Most of us tend to underplay our triumphs for we are taught as children not to boast—to be nice and humble and call upon the Lord for forgiveness of our wretched state. That is a bunch of spiritual hogwash. You do not have to fake being humble and the Lord does not consider you wretched at all. Even in your most awful moments you are beautiful, and eternity is laced through every molecule of your being.

As you begin to see your life as important, each and every act, however small, becomes important as well. So a walk in silence at dawn is a triumph of discipline, an affirmation of essence. Giving your notice at work may be another. An hour communicating with a person who is causing you trouble is another. Once you focus on success, the things you do toward that end act like candles on your path. Affirmations of essence help you notice the candles.

Your affirmations of essence become signposts in your life. They act as triggers that release positive energy stored within you.

As you stake out the parts of your life that are strong, they will assist you to become even stronger. Take time to honor those strongholds: the love you have for your family and friends, your love of nature, your ability to earn a consistent living, your creative power, your sharp wit or whatever. When, on rare occasions you come out of an energy that is less than best, take a moment to look at why you did that, then shrug it off. Never harp on what has gone before and never harp on what people feel you did or did not do. By looking at the signposts of your life, you weave a pattern of strength all around you. Choose people that enhance this and use their energy. Pick places that feel powerful, go there and notice the power they give you. If an experience comes along that is unusually strong, mark it down in your mind and recreate it at a later date in your feelings, or at least have a strong memory pattern that you can re-call at any time.

Select the strongest path at all times. In walking into a restaurant there will be weak and strong spots. Use your feelings to select the highest possible energy at all times. Do not let fate wield you, you wield fate. Ambience, color, music, food— all are decisions to be made by you. Never say, "I do not know," for that is not usually correct. If the sage does not know, he or she pulls back and reviews the feeling, reviews the strength and soon the answer comes.

Spend as little time as possible in the distractions of life and as much time as possible moving toward your goal. Feel free to cut people short if they waste your time. Eliminate all unneccesary effort and try to maximize your own free time—time that you will use to better your life, to study, to learn, to indulge in life— time to understand yourself and time to honor the Life Force in all things.

The cult of the individual will inherit the earth, for in the end everyone will see that this is the only path and that all associations are but way-stations to the individual transcendence that is the destiny of us all. Make your choices, then feel free to change them if you wish. But make choices.

Become action-oriented, collect valuable experiences and use those experiences to assist you in surmounting the next challenge. Develop plans, write the storyboard of your life and follow it.

Move deliberately, walk don't run, and as you do so get used to noticing the world around you.

Your expectations are limitless and affirmations of action will serve as the culmination of your dreams delivered in the physical. You will find that your life moves in phases and that you will be offered the chance to complete each phase. Tie up the loose ends, pay your debts, reconcile your relationships. The closing out on one allows you to move to another. Complete your obligations and be careful not to take on any more unless they serve you. Allow yourself as much fluidity as possible. In doing so you speed up the energy of your life and you will find that you complete projects even more quickly.

Creativity is basically a spark of the universal mind, transformed by you into action. The closer you are to the light, the less complicated your life. The less opinions you have, the more energy flows. I have seen people reach prolific creativity almost overnight by aligning their life to power and taking action within the context of their intentions.

Once you hone your energy down to a fine point of concentration, the Universal Law responds quickly for there is nothing to clutter the delivery system. The more you dominate in your world and leave the world of others alone, the more you will win the support of the God Force, the more you will feel that you can triumph over all circumstances.

You can never know *all* the answers. No matter how powerful you become, the great mysteries of life will always hover just out of reach. When you see beauty, move toward it; when you see ugliness, move away. That is your affirmation of essence. Eventually the immortality you seek will inexorably become a part of your existence.

As you learn to trust the power within you, it responds. It is as if in the act of trusting your fate to the God Force within you, you create a vulnerability that keeps you safe. The man in the street is vulnerable because he does not know what he is doing and he suffers from thinking he knows it all. The sage is vulnerable because, in his benign love for all things, he opens himself to all things and so his vulnerability keeps him safe, for his energy is not of the ego, it is an energy of transcendence and respect. The sage knows he knows nothing.

As we move out of this millenium into the twenty-first century you will see a great splitting of mankind, not a coming together. Those with power and discipline will forge ahead to culminate their efforts in one last flowering of human endeavor. Others will fall back and re-enter tribalism, a modern version perhaps, but tribalism just the same. And that is what is meant to be.

The world will cry out in its anguish and you — all evil shed away, a molecule in the eternity of all things — will stand for the benefit of mankind. You will be a representative of a celestial state, little understood and even less acknowledged to administer a kindness, a healing that asks nothing in return. Once you have given of yourself in love and softness your actions will stand around you like old friends. The energy that expresses powerfully from within will reclaim you back to rest in the exquisite beauty of all things, reunited at last in peace and gentleness, truly able to say unto yourself, "I am eternal, immortal, universal and infinite. So be it."

The Warrior's Prayer

I am what I am.

In having faith in the beauty within me,
I develop trust.

In softness I have strength.

In silence I walk with the gods.

In peace I understand myself and the world.

In conflict I walk away.

In detachment I am free.

In respecting all living things, I respect myself.

In dedication I honor the courage within me.

In eternity I have compassion for the nature of all things.

In love I unconditionally accept the evolution of others.

In freedom I have power.

In my individuality I express the God Force within me.

In service I give of what I have become.

I am what I am:

Eternal, immortal, universal and infinite.

And so be it.

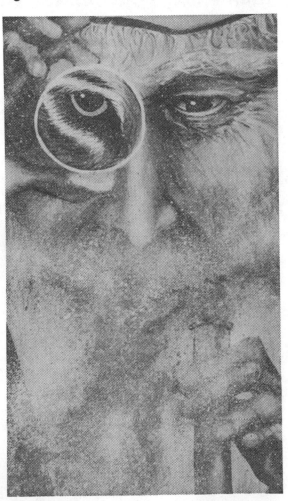

BOOKS BY STUART WILDE

Affirmations

Most of the organizations and structures in the world are designed to take away your power. *Affirmations* serves not so much to give you nice words to say to yourself, but rather as a magnificent battle-plan, where you learn to expand the power you already have to win back absolute control of your life. This is the only true spiritual path. Everything else is just a way station, while you gather enough confidence to step out on your own. You need your power back now. And to do so, you will have to become like a 'gorilla on the path' that will walk up to the system and lovingly demand its bone back!

Miracles

Understanding miracles is no more complicated than understanding the metaphysics of the Universal Law.

To create miracles, you have to be very clear about what you want. Then you have to hold the warrior's thought: you are going to reach your goal, no matter what confronts you, no matter where you are right now; nothing is going to be allowed to bump you off your course. By being forthright and acting as if you already have obtained the object or condition that you desire, you create such a powerful energy that the Universal Law gives you what you want.
Excerpted from **Miracles**.

The Force

The Force, like your Higher Self, is an energy that experiences evolution. It is massive, exhilirating, magnanimous beyond description—perhaps you might want to call it God. It is not stagnant, as some would have you believe. It is growing, dynamic and has an inner drive or desire to become more of itself. To achieve this, it divides itself into more and more separate parts or definitions, and it does so because it knows that, by dividing and spreading out, it will have more power and, having more power, it will grow.

The Force is the inner light or "livingness" in all things. The more Life Force a thing expresses, the more complicated or greater is the Force within it. Therefore, a small bird expresses more of the Force than does a rock and a human being expresses still more than a bird.

But everything has the Force within it and that is the key to an individual's understanding...
Excerpted from **The Force**.

USE THE CONVENIENT FORM BELOW TO ORDER BY MAIL OR CONTACT YOUR LOCAL BOOKSTORE.